THE PENGUIN POETS

D 31

MORE COMIC AND CURIOUS

VERSE

MORE COMIC
AND CURIOUS VERSE

COLLECTED BY

J. M. Cohen

PENGUIN BOOKS

Penguin Books Ltd, Harmondsworth, Middlesex
AUSTRALIA: Penguin Books Pty Ltd, 762 Whitehorse Road,
Mitcham, Victoria

—

First published 1956
Reprinted 1958, 1960, 1964

—

This selection copyright © J. M. Cohen, 1956

—

Made and printed in Great Britain
by The Whitefriars Press Ltd,
London and Tonbridge
Set in Monotype Fournier

Cover design by Stephen Russ

To my son
Philip

Contents

Foreword

THE collection for this second rag-bag of *Comic and Curious Verse* began from the moment that the first was packed up for the printers. There were, necessarily, pieces left out that I should greatly liked to include, and so for some months there lay in a folder a batch of poems that had just failed to fit into the stipulated length. Among these was 'The Hunting of the Snark', which would have been entirely spoiled by cutting but which would have forced out many of my less known finds if I had put it in complete. Soon this folder was swelled by my newspaper critics and correspondents. *Wot, no Byron? ... But, why did you not put in* this, that or the other? The field of comic verse is very wide, and there was a great deal which others had treasured and could repeat from memory that I had never even seen. But when, this year, Penguins asked me to fill the bag again, things went from good to better. For not only did the libraries prove to possess collections that were quite new to me, but many friends began to offer heaven-sent suggestions. Did I know X, who wrote the best nonsense verse of the present day? Poems by X are included in this book. Did I know that some brilliant translations of the Austrian, Christian Morgenstern, had been done before the war by R. F. C. Hull, and were lying unprinted in a drawer? I had very much wanted to include Morgenstern in the first *Comic and Curious*, but had seen no good versions in English. So readers will find here, for the first time, a fair selection from the poems of the sly and whimsical inventor of Palmström and Korf, who is, in my opinion, the equal of Carroll or Lear. Then Michael Hamburger undertook a few more translations of favourite pieces that have never been seen in English dress. So, the new book will be found to contain just as much unfamiliar material as the first — perhaps even more.

I have set myself roughly the same terms of reference as last time, and assembled my poems under eight headings: 'Odd Voices', 'Doubtful Tales', 'Squints at Nature', 'Tricks and Teases', 'Mockery and Invective', 'Studied Irreverence', 'Ballads to Harp Accompaniment', and 'Short Measure'. Perhaps this time there is a little more satire than before, but otherwise the mixture is, I think, much the same, and the strength of the brew, I believe, not a penn'orth weaker; nothing that I rejected last time has found its way into this second book. I have, however, put in several pieces by Lewis Carroll, Lear, and Calverley, which deserved places, but could not have gone in without throwing the balance of the book badly out. I have made some fresh choices from that neglected master, Thomas Hood, crammed in two *Ingoldsby Legends* and offered the brothers Horace and James Smith, whom I overlooked in 1950, some small amends. Again I have limited myself more or less to poems written since 1700, and again I have interpreted the term 'curious' in my own way, thus granting myself licence to include the ballad 'Wednesbury Cocking', for instance, a good bit of Midland knockabout, and the 'Rhyme of the Rusher', the best poem I have seen in Cockney rhyming slang, also sundry other playful poems in the section 'Tricks and Teases'. The selection is a personal one, and will no doubt contain a pet *dislike* or two of every reader's; I hope that it also contains sufficient *likes* to compensate him and her, and them.

This time I have not drawn to any considerable extent on existing anthologies. I have seen only one new one since my first *Comic and Curious*, the late Arnold Silcock's very individual *Verse and Worse*, from which I have drawn half-a-dozen small anonymous pieces that I had never seen elsewhere, and one poignant little pastoral by the anthologist himself. My debt is not to other collections but to various friends, some of whom I know only from correspondence or the telephone, for poems, recommendations, and disquisitions on the art of Comic Verse. These include John Dobell, Professor L. W. Forster, Derek Hudson, R. F. C. Hull, Terence Kilmartin, Marghanita Laski, Professor C. S. Lewis, A. G. Prys-Jones, John Ross, Edward Upward, and Douglas Webster. The help, secretarial, advisory, and admonitory, that I have received from my son Philip is, I hope, sufficiently acknowledged by my dedication. My wife's judgement, which has often tipped the scales in favour of inclusion or exclusion, has been as helpful to me here as in other fields of literary work. I have grown so used to relying on it that this brief acknowledgement is an absurdly inadequate return for her patience and her sound good sense.

J.M.C.

ACKNOWLEDGEMENTS

For permission to reprint copyright matter, the following acknowledgements are made:

For a poem by W. H. Auden, from *From the Time being*, to the author and Messrs Faber & Faber Ltd; for poems by Hilaire Belloc from *Cautionary Verses* and *Sonnets and Verse*, to the author's executors and Messrs George Duckworth Ltd; to E. K Bennett and Nicolas Bentley, each for one clerihew; for three poems by Morris Bishop, from *A Bowl of Bishop*, to the author and The Dial Press Inc.; for one poem by G. W. Brodribb, from *Poems*, to the author's executor and Messrs Macmillan & Co. Ltd; for one poem by Harry Brown from *Poems*, to the author and Messrs Secker & Warburg Ltd; for a poem by Gerald Bullett, first published in *Punch*, to the author and the proprietors of *Punch*; for one poem by S. J. Cohen, to the author; for six poems by Alan Crick, to the author; for one poem by Colin Curzon, from *Flying Wild* (Hurst & Blackett), to the author; for two poems by David Daiches, which originally appeared in *The New Yorker*, to the author; for two poems by Walter de la Mare, from *Peacock Pie* and *Collected Rhymes and Verses*, to the author and Messrs Faber & Faber Ltd; for one poem by Patric Dickinson, to the author; for one poem by Irwin Edman, to the late author and *The New Yorker*; for one poem by T. S. Eliot, from *Old Possum's Book of Practical Cats*, to Messrs Faber & Faber Ltd, and the author; for one poem by Mrs J. E. Faulks, to the authoress; for two poems by Sir W. S. Gilbert, from *The Bab Ballads*, to Miss Nancy McIntosh and Messrs Macmillan & Co. Ltd; for one poem by Harry Graham from *The World we laugh in*, to the author's executrix and Messrs Methuen & Co. Ltd, and for one of his *Ruthless Rhymes*, and two of his *More Ruthless Rhymes*, to the author's executrix and Messrs Edward Arnold Ltd; for two poems by Arthur Guiterman, one from *Lyric Laughter* and one from *Gaily the Troubadour*, to the author and Messrs E. P. Dutton & Co. Inc.; for two poems and four translations by Michael Hamburger to the author; for ten translations by R. F. C. Hull, to the author; for one poem by Phyllis McGinley, from *A Short Walk from the Station*, first published in *The New Yorker*, to the authoress and The Viking Press Inc.; for two poems by H. S. Mackintosh from *Ballades and other verse*, to the author and Messrs Rupert Hart-Davis Ltd; for a poem by Don Marquis, from *Archy's Life of Mehitabel*, to the author's executors and Messrs Faber & Faber Ltd; for one poem by James Michie, to the author; for five poems by J. B. Morton ('Beach-comber' of the *Daily Express*), to the author; for ten poems by Ogden Nash, from *Family Reunion* and *The Private Dining Room*, to the author and Messrs J. M. Dent & Sons Ltd; for one poem by W. Plomer from *The Dorking Thigh*, to the author and Messrs Jonathan Cape Ltd; for one poem by E. Powys Mathers, to the author's executors and the Imago Press; for five poems by A. G. Prys-Jones, to the author; for one poem by Sir A. Quiller-Couch, to the author's executrix and Messrs J. M. Dent & Sons Ltd; for six pieces by A. B. Ramsay from *Flos Malvae* and *Frondes Salicis*, to the late author and the Cambridge University Press; for one piece by Justin Richardson, to the author and for another to the author and the proprietors of *Punch;* for a poem by G. W. E. Russell, from *A Londoner's Log Book*, to the author's executors and Messrs John Murray; for one poem by Arnold Silcock from his anthology, *Verse and Worse* (Faber & Faber), to the author's executors; for two poems by Dame Edith Sitwell, from *Façade*, to the authoress and Messrs George Duckworth Ltd; for one poem by Sir Osbert Sitwell, from *Wreck at Tidesend*, to the author and Messrs Macmillan & Co. Ltd; for two poems by K. M. Stern, from *Gemixte Pickles*, to the author and Crown Publishers Inc.; for two poems by G. Taylor to the author; for one poem by J. G. C. Trench to the author and Messrs Arthur Guiness, Son & Co. Ltd; for two poems by G. A. Vallins, from *Sincere Flattery*, to the author, the Epworth Press and the proprietors of *Punch*, in which they first appeared; for one translation by Doctor Arthur Waley, from *Chinese Poems*, to the author and Messrs Allen & Unwin Ltd; and for seven poems by D. B. Wyndham Lewis to the author. In addition to the pieces already credited to them, the proprietors of *Punch* have given permission for the inclusion of work by P. Barrington, M. Bevan, J. B. Boothroyd, Peter Dickinson, A. Hall, P. M. Hubbard, E. V. Knox, K. Lillington, M. H. Longson, R. Mallett, D. Mattam, Sir Owen Seaman, and R. E. C. Stringer, all of which originally appeared in their journal. In addition they have kindly traced the authorship of the poem 'Merry May', which they published a century ago.

Thanks are also due to Dr E. V. Rieu for one poem, and to Phyllis McGinley, and Messrs J. M. Dent & Son Ltd, for one piece from *The Love Letters of Phyllis McGinley*.

It has been impossible to find the authors of several poems that have been included, or to be certain that their work is out of copyright. Apologies are offered for any such unintentional discourtesy.

J . M . C .

ODD VOICES

To Sally, at the Chop-House

Dear Sally, emblem of the chop-house ware,
As broth reviving, and as white bread fair;
As small beer grateful, and as pepper strong,
As beef-steak tender, as fresh pot-herbs young;
Sharp as a knife, and piercing as a fork,
Soft as new butter, white as fairest pork;
Sweet as young mutton, brisk as bottled beer,
Smooth as is oil, juicy as cucumber,
And bright as cruet void of vinegar.
O Sally! could I turn and shift my love
With the same skill that you your steaks can move,
My heart, thus cooked, might prove a chop-house feast,
And you alone should be the welcome guest.
But, dearest Sal, the flames that you impart,
Like chop on gridiron, broil my tender heart!
Which, if thy kindly helping hand be n't nigh,
Must, like an up-turned chop, hiss, brown and fry;
And must at last, thou scorcher of my soul,
Shrink, and become an undistinguished coal.

ANON.

A Pinch of Snuff

Who does not know what logic lies concealed
Where diving finger meets with diving thumb?
Who hath not seen the opponent fly the field,
Unhurt by argument, by snuff struck dumb?

The box drawn forth from its profoundest bed,
The slow-repeated tap, with frowning brows,
The brandished pinch, the fingers widely spread,
The arm tossed round returning to the nose.

Who can withstand a battery so strong?
Wit, reason, learning, what are ye to these?
Or who could toil through folios thick and long,
When wisdom may be purchased with a sneeze?

ANON.

A Parental Ode to my Son, aged Three Years and Five Months

Thou happy, happy elf!
(But stop – first let me kiss away that tear) –
Thou tiny image of myself!
(My love, he's poking peas into his ear!)
Thou merry, laughing sprite!
With spirits feather-light,
Untouch'd by sorrow, and unsoil'd by sin –
(Good heavens! the child is swallowing a pin!)

Thou little tricksy Puck!
With antic toys so funnily bestuck,
Light as the singing bird that wings the air –
(The door! the door! he'll tumble down the stair!)
Thou darling of thy sire!
(Why, Jane, he'll set his pinafore a-fire!)
Thou imp of mirth and joy!
In love's dear chain so strong and bright a link,
Thou idol of thy parents – (drat the boy!
there goes my ink!)

Thou cherub – but of earth;
Fit playfellow for Fays by moonlight pale,
In harmless sport and mirth,
(That dog will bite him if he pulls its tail!)
Thou human humming-bee, extracting honey
From every blossom in the world that blows,
Singing in Youth's Elysium ever sunny –
(Another tumble! – that's his precious nose!)

Thy father's pride and hope!
(He'll break the mirror with that skipping-rope!)
With pure heart newly stamp'd from nature's mint,
    (Where *did* he learn that squint?)
    Thou young domestic dove!
(He'll have that jug off, with another shove!)
    Dear nursling of the hymeneal nest!
    (Are those torn clothes his best?)
    Little epitome of man!
(He'll climb upon the table, that's his plan!)
Touch'd with the beauteous tints of dawning life,
    (He's got a knife!)

    Thou enviable being!
No storms, no clouds, in the blue sky foreseeing,
    Play on, play on,
    My elfin John!
Toss the light ball – bestride the stick –
(I knew so many cakes would make him sick!)
With fancies buoyant as the thistledown,
Prompting the face grotesque, and antic brisk,
    With many a lamb-like frisk –
(He's got the scissors, snipping at your gown!)

    Thou pretty opening rose!
(Go to your mother, child, and wipe your nose!)
Balmy, and breathing music like the South,
(He really brings my heart into my mouth!)
Fresh as the morn, and brilliant as its star –
(I wish that window had an iron bar!)
Bold as a hawk, yet gentle as the dove –
    (I'll tell you what, my love,
I cannot write unless he's sent above!)

THOMAS HOOD

Ode to Madame Hengler

FIREWORK-MAKER TO VAUXHALL

Oh, Mrs Hengler! – Madame, – I beg your pardon;
Starry Enchantress of the Surrey Garden!
Accept an Ode not meant as any scoff –
The Bard were bold indeed at thee to quiz,
Whose squibs are far more popular than his;
Whose works are much more certain to go off.

Great is thy fame, but not a silent fame;
With many a bang the public ear it courts;
And yet thy arrogance we never blame,
But take thy merits from thy own reports.
Thou hast indeed the most indulgent backers,
We make no doubting, misbelieving comments,
Even in thy most bounceable of moments;
But lend our ears implicit to thy crackers! –
Strange helps to thy applause too are not missing,
        Thy Rockets raise thee,
        And Serpents praise thee,
As none beside are ever praised – by hissing!

        Mistress of Hydropyrics,
Of glittering Pindarics, Sapphics, Lyrics,
Professor of a Fiery Necromancy,
Oddly thou charmest the politer sorts
        With midnight sports,
Partaking very much of *flash* and *fancy*!

        What thoughts had shaken all
In olden time at thy nocturnal revels, –
        Each brimstone ball
They would have deem'd an eyeball of the Devil's!

But now thy flaming meteors cause no fright;
A modern Hubert to the royal ear
      Might whisper without fear,
'My Lord, they say there were five moons to-night!'
Nor would it raise one superstitious notion
To hear the whole description fairly out: —
'One fixed — which t'other four whirl'd round about
      With wond'rous motion.'

      Such are the very sights
Thou workest, Queen of Fire, on earth and heaven,
Between the hours of midnight and eleven,
Turning our English to Arabian Nights,
With blazing mounts, and founts, and scorching dragons,
      Blue stars and white,
      And blood-red light,
And dazzling wheels fit for Enchanters' wagons.
Thrice lucky woman! doing things that be
With other folks past benefit of parson;
For burning, no Burn's Justice falls on thee,
Altho' night after night the public see
The Vauxhall palaces all end in Arson!

      Sure thou wast never born
Like old Sir Hugh, with water in thy head,
      Nor lectur'd night and morn
Of sparks and flames to have an awful dread,
Allowed by a prophetic dam and sire
      To play with fire.
O didst thou never, in those days gone by,
Go carrying about — no schoolboy prouder —
Instead of waxen doll a little Guy;
Or in thy pretty pyrotechnic vein,
Up the parental pigtail lay a train,
      To let off all his powder?

Full of the wildfire of thy youth
            Did'st never in plain truth,
Plant whizzing Flowers in thy mother's pots,
Turning the garden into powder plots?
            Or give the cook, to fright her,
Thy paper sausages well stuffed with nitre?
Nay, wert thou never guilty, now, of dropping
A lighted cracker by the sister's Dear,
            So that she could not hear
            The question he was popping?

Go on, Madame! Go on – be bright and busy
While hoax'd Astronomers look up and stare
From tall observatories, dumb and dizzy,
To see a Squib in Cassiopeia's Chair!
A Serpent wriggling into Charles's Wain!
A Roman Candle lighting the Great Bear!
A Rocket tangled in Diana's train,
And Crackers stuck in Berenice's Hair!

There is a King of Fire – Thou shouldst be Queen!
Methinks a good connexion might come from it;
Could'st thou not make him, in the garden scene,
Set out per Rocket and return per Comet;
            Then give him a hot treat
Of Pyrotechnicals to sit and sup,
Lord! how the world would throng to see him eat,
He swallowing fire, while thou dost throw it up!

One solitary night – true is the story –
Watching those forms that fancy will create
Within the bright confusion of the gate,
I saw a dazzling countenance of glory!
            Oh Dei gratias!
            That fiery facias

'Twas thine, Enchantress of the Surrey Grove;
　　And ever since that night,
　　In dark and bright,
Thy face is *registered* within my *stove!*

Long may that starry brow enjoy its rays;
May no untimely *blow* its doom forestall;
But when old age prepares the friendly pall,
When the last spark of all thy sparks decays,
Then die lamented by good people all,
　　Like Goldsmith's *Madam Blaize!*

THOMAS HOOD

Next-door Neighbours

My wife and I live *comme il faut,*
At number Six in Crosby Row;
　　So few our household labours,
We quickly turn from joints and pies,
To use two tongues and twice two eyes
　　To meliorate our neighbours.

My eye-glass, thanks to Dollond's skill,
Sweeps up the lane to Mears's Mill,
　　While, latticed in her chamber,
My wife peeps through her window-pane,
To note who ramble round the lane,
　　And who the foot-stile clamber.

This morn the zig-zag man of meat
Trotted, tray-balanced, up the street –
　　We saw him halt at Sydney's:
My wife asserts he left lamb there;
But I myself can all but swear
　　'Twas mutton-chops and kidneys.

The man who goes about with urns
Is beckon'd in by Betty Burns:
　　The poor girl knows no better:
But Mrs Burns should have more sense;
That broken tray is mere pretence –
　　He brings the girl a letter.

Whether she goes up street for milk,
Or brings home sugar, pins, or silk,
　　That silly wench for ever
Draws up, pretending at the stile
To rest herself, while all the while
　　She waits for Captain Trevor.

The captain, when he sees me, turns,
Seems not to notice Betty Burns,
　　And round the pond betakes him,
Behind the stables of the Bear,
To get the back way in; but there
　　My wife's back window rakes him.

There go the Freaks again – but hark!
I hear the gate-bell ring – 'tis Bark,
　　The glib apothecary,
Who in his mortar pounds the fame
Of every rumour-wounded dame,
　　From Moll to Lady Mary.

'Well, Mr Bark,' – 'I've found her out.'
'Who is she?' – 'Not his wife.' – 'No doubt.'
　　''Twas told me by his brother.'
'Which brother? Archibald?' – 'No Fred,
An old connexion.' – 'So I said.'
　　'The woman's – ' 'What?' – 'His mother.'

'Who are the comers next to Blake's?'
'At number Four?' – 'Yes.' – 'No great shakes:
    Sad junketings and wastings.
I've seen them play in "Days of Yore",
He acted Hastings in Jane Shore,
    And she Jane Shore in Hastings.'

'Pray Mr Bark, what party drove
That dark-brown chariot to the Grove?'
    'The Perrys, Ma'am, wet Quakers.
He married Mrs Hartley Grant,
Whose father's uncle's mother's aunt
    Liv'd cook at Lady Dacre's.'

But Sunday is the time, of course,
When Gossip's congregated force
    Pours from our central chapel:
Then hints and anecdotes increase,
And in the Mansion-house of Peace
    Dark Discord drops her apple.

Ope but a casement, turn a lock,
The whole row feels th' electric shock,
    Springs tilt, their blinds up throwing,
And every ear and every eye
Darts to one centre, to descry
    Who's coming or who's going.

Thus occupied in Crosby Row,
We covet not the Grange or Stowe;
    Pent in by walls and palings,
Their lordly tenants can't, like us,
Drop in at tea-time to discuss
    Their neighbours' faults and failings.

JAMES SMITH

Private Theatricals

LADY ARABELLA FUSTIAN TO LORD CLARENCE FUSTIAN

> — Sweet when Actors first appear,
> The loud collision of applauding gloves!
> MOULTRIE

Your labours, my talented brother,
  Are happily over at last;
They tell me that, somehow or other,
  The Bill is rejected – or past:
And now you'll be coming, I'm certain,
  As fast as four posters can crawl,
To help us to draw up our curtain,
  As usual, at Fustian Hall.

Arrangements are nearly completed;
  But still we've a lover or two,
Whom Lady Albina entreated
  We'd keep, at all hazards, for you:
Sir Arthur makes horrible faces –
  Lord John is a trifle too tall –
And yours are the safest embraces
  To faint in, at Fustian Hall.

Come, Clarence; – it's really enchanting
  To listen and look at the rout;
We're all of us puffing, and panting,
  And raving, and running about;
Here Kitty and Adelaide bustle;
  There Andrew and Antony bawl;
Flutes murmur, chains rattle, robes rustle,
  In chorus, at Fustian Hall.

Bye the bye, there are two or three matters
  We want you to bring us from Town;

The Inca's white plumes from the hatter's,
 A nose and a hump for the clown:
We want a few harps at our banquet;
 We want a few masques for our ball;
And steal from your wise friend Bosanquet
 His white wig, for Fustian Hall.

Huncamunca must have a huge sabre,
 Friar Tuck has forgotten his cowl;
And we're quite at a standstill with Weber,
 For want of a lizard and owl:
And then, for our funeral procession,
 Pray give us a love of a pall;
Or how shall we make an impression
 On feelings at Fustian Hall?

And, Clarence, you'll really delight us,
 If you'll do your endeavour to bring
From the Club a young person to write us
 Our prologue, and that sort of thing;
Poor Crotchet, who did them supremely
 Is gone, for a Judge, to Bengal;
I fear we shall miss him extremely
 This season, at Fustian Hall.

Come, Clarence – your idol Albina
 Will make a sensation, I feel;
We all think there never was seen a
 Performer so like the O'Neill:
At rehearsals, her exquisite fury
 Has deeply affected us all;
For one tear that trickles at Drury,
 There'll be twenty at Fustian Hall.

Dread objects are scattered before her,
 On purpose to harrow her soul;

She stares, till a deep spell comes o'er her,
    At a knife, or a cross, or a bowl.
The sword never seems to alarm her,
    That hangs on a peg to the wall;
And she doats on thy rusty old armour,
    Lord Fustian, of Fustian Hall.

She stabbed a bright mirror this morning –
    Poor Kitty was quite out of breath –
And trampled in anger and scorning,
    A bonnet and feathers to death.
But hark – I've a part in 'The Stranger' –
    There's the Prompter's detestable call:
Come, Clarence – our Romeo and Ranger,
    We want you at Fustian Hall.

                                    W. M. PRAED

Mr Molony's Account of the Ball

GIVEN TO THE NEPAULESE AMBASSADOR BY THE
PENINSULAR AND ORIENTAL COMPANY

O Will ye choose to hear the news,
    Bedad I cannot pass it o'er:
I'll tell you all about the Ball
    To the Naypaulase Ambassador.
Begor! this fête all balls does bate
    At which I've worn a pump, and I
Must here relate the splendthor great
    Of th' Oriental Company.

These men of sinse dispoised expinse,
    To fête these black Achilleses.
'We'll show the blacks,' says they, 'Almack's,
    And take the rooms at Willis's.'
With flags and shawls, for these Nepauls,
    They hung the rooms of Willis up,

And decked the walls, and stairs, and halls,
  With roses and with lilies up.

And Jullien's band it tuck its stand
  So sweetly in the middle there,
And soft bassoons played heavenly chunes,
  And violins did fiddle there.
And when the Coort was tired of spoort,
  I'd lave you, boys, to think there was
A nate buffet before them set,
  Where lashins of good dthrink there was.

At ten before the ballroom door,
  His moighty Excellency was,
He smoiled and bowed to all the crowd,
  So gorgeous and immense he was.
His dusky shuit, sublime and mute,
  Into the doorway followed him;
And O the noise of the blackguard boys,
  As they hurrood and hollowed him!

The noble Chair stud at the stair,
  And bade the dthrums to thump; and he
Did thus evince, to that Black Prince,
  The welcome of his Company.
O fair the girls, and rich the curls,
  And bright the oys you saw there was,
And fixed each oye, ye there could spoi,
  On Gineral Jung Bahawther, was!

This Gineral great then tuck his sate,
  With all the other ginerals
(Bedad his troat, his belt, his coat,
  All bleezed with precious minerals);
And as he there, with princely air,
  Recloinin on his cushion was,

All round about his royal chair
   The squeezin and the pushin was.

O Pat, such girls, such Jukes, and Earls,
   Such fashion and nobilitee!
Just think of Tim, and fancy him
   Amidst the hoigh gentilitee!
There was Lord De L'Huys, and the Portygeese
   Ministher and his lady there,
And I reckonized, with much surprise,
   Our messmate, Bob O'Grady, there;

There was Baroness Brunow, that looked like Juno,
   And Baroness Rehausen there,
And Countess Roullier, that looked peculiar
   Well, in her robes of gauze in there.
There was Lord Crowhurst (I knew him first,
   When only Mr Pips he was),
And Mick O'Toole, the great big fool,
   That after supper tipsy was.

There was Lord Fingall, and his ladies all,
   And Lords Killeen and Dufferin,
And Paddy Fife, with his fat wife;
   I wondther how he could stuff her in.
There was Lord Belfast, that by me past,
   And seemed to ask how should I go there?
And the Widow Macrae, and Lord A. Hay,
   And the Marchioness of Sligo there.

Yes, Jukes, and Earls, and diamonds, and pearls,
   And pretty girls, was spoorting there;
And some beside (the rogues!) I spied,
   Behind the windies, coorting there.
O, there's one I know, bedad, would show
   As beautiful as any there,

And I'd like to hear the pipers blow,
  And shake a fut with Fanny there!

                        W. M. THACKERAY

The Palace

They come, they come, with fife and drum,
  And gleaming pikes and glancing banners:
Though the eyes flash, the lips are dumb;
  To talk in rank would not be manners.
Onward they stride, as Britons can;
The ladies following in the van.

Who, who be these that tramp in threes
  Through sumptuous Piccadilly, through
The roaring Strand, and stand at ease
  At last 'neath shadowy Waterloo?
Some gallant Guild, I ween, are they;
Taking their annual holiday.

To catch the destin'd train – to pay
  Their willing fares, and plunge within it –
Is, as in old Romaunt they say,
  With them the work of half-a-minute.
Then off they're whirl'd, with songs and shouting,
To cedared Sydenham for their outing.

I mark'd them light, with faces bright
  As pansies or a new coin'd florin,
And up the sunless stair take flight,
  Close pack'd as rabbits in a warren.
Honour the Brave, who in that stress
Still trod not upon Beauty's dress!

Kerchief in hand I saw them stand;
    In every kerchief lurk'd a lunch;
When they unfurl'd them, it was grand
    To watch bronzed men and maidens crunch
The sounding celery-stick, or ram
The knife into the blushing ham.

Dash'd the bold fork through pies of pork;
    O'er hard-boil'd eggs the saltspoon shook;
Leapt from its lair the playful cork;
    Yet some there were to whom the brook
Seem'd sweetest beverage, and for meat
They chose the red root of the beet.

But ah! what bard could sing how hard,
    The artless banquet o'er, they ran
Down the soft slope with daisies starr'd
    And kingcups! onward, maid with man,
They flew, to scale the breezy swing,
Or court frank kisses in the ring.

Such are the sylvan scenes that thrill
    This heart! The lawns, the happy shade,
Where matrons, whom the sunbeams grill,
    Stir with slow spoon their lemonade;
And maidens flirt (no extra charge)
In comfort at the fountain's marge!

Others may praise the 'grand displays'
    Where 'fiery arch', 'cascade' and 'comet'.
Set the whole garden in a 'blaze'!
    Far, at such times, may I be from it;
Though then the public may be 'lost
In wonder' at a trifling cost.

Fann'd by the breeze, to puff at ease
  My faithful pipe is all I crave:
And if folks rave about the 'trees
  Lit up by fireworks', let them rave.
Your monster fêtes, I like not these;
Though they bring grist to the lessees.

                              C. S. CALVERLEY

Companions

A TALE OF A GRANDFATHER

I know not of what we ponder'd
  Or made pretty pretence to talk,
As, her hand within mine, we wander'd
  Tow'rd the pool by the limetree walk,
While the dew fell in showers from the passion flowers
  And the blush-rose bent on her stalk.

I cannot recall her figure:
  Was it regal as Juno's own?
Or only a trifle bigger
  Than the elves who surround the throne
Of the Faery Queen, and are seen, I ween,
  By mortals in dreams alone?

What her eyes were like, I know not:
  Perhaps they were blurr'd with tears;
And perhaps in your skies there glow not
  (On the contrary) clearer spheres.
No! as to her eyes I am just as wise
  As you or the cat, my dears.

Her teeth, I presume, were 'pearly':
    But which was she, brunette or blonde?
Her hair, was it quaintly curly,
    Or as straight as a beadle's wand?
That I fail'd to remark: – it was rather dark
    And shadowy round the pond.

Then the hand that reposed so snugly
    In mine – was it plump or spare?
Was the countenance fair or ugly?
    Nay, children, you have me there!
My eyes were p'raps blurr'd: and besides I'd heard
    That it's horribly rude to stare.

And I – was I brusque and surly?
    Or oppressively bland and fond?
Was I partial to rising early?
    Or why did we twain abscond,
All breakfastless too, from the public view
    To prowl by a misty pond?

What pass'd, what was felt or spoken –
    Whether anything pass'd at all –
And whether the heart was broken
    That beat under that shelt'ring shawl –
(If shawl she had on, which I doubt) – has gone,
    Yes, gone from me past recall.

Was I haply the lady's suitor?
    Or her uncle? I can't make out –
Ask your governess, dears, or tutor.
    For myself, I'm in hopeless doubt
As to why we were there, who on earth we were,
    And what this is all about.

                              C. S. CALVERLEY

The Twins

In form and feature, face and limb,
  I grew so like my brother
That folks got taking me for him
  And each for one another.
It puzzled all our kith and kin,
  It reach'd an awful pitch;
For one of us was born a twin
  And not a soul knew which.

One day (to make the matter worse),
  Before our names were fix'd,
As we were being washed by nurse,
  We got completely mix'd.
And thus, you see, by Fate's decree,
  (Or rather nurse's whim)
My brother John got christened *me*,
  And I got christened *him*.

This fatal likeness even dogg'd
  My footsteps when at school,
And I was always getting flogg'd —
  For John turn'd out a fool.
I put this question hopelessly
  To everyone I knew —
What *would* you do if you were *me*,
  To prove that you were *you*?

Our close resemblance turned the tide
  Of my domestic life;
For somehow my intended bride
  Became my brother's wife.
In short, year after year the same
  Absurd mistakes went on;

And when I died – the neighbours came
And buried brother John!

H. S. LEIGH

On Photographs

She played me false, but that's not why
I haven't quite forgiven Di,
    Although I've tried.
This curl was hers, so brown, so bright,
She gave it me one blissful night,
    And – more beside.

In photo we were grouped together.
She wore the darling hat and feather
    That I adore:
In profile by her side I sat,
Reading my poetry – but that
    She'd heard before.

Why, after all, Di threw me over
I never knew, and can't discover,
    Or even guess:
Maybe Smith's lyrics, she decided,
Were sweeter than the sweetest I did –
    I acquiesce.

A week before their wedding-day
When Smith was called in haste away
    To join the Staff,
Di gave to him, with tearful mien,
Our only photograph. I've seen
    That photograph.

I've seen it in Smith's album-book!
Just think! her hat – her tender look,
    Are now that brute's!
Before she gave it, off she cut
My body, head and lyrics, but
She was obliged, the little slut,
    To leave my boots.

FREDERICK LOCKER LAMPSON

Turtle Soup

Beautiful Soup, so rich and green,
    Waiting in a hot tureen!
Who for such dainties would not stoop?
Soup of the evening, beautiful Soup!
Soup of the evening, beautiful Soup!
    Beau-ootiful Soo-oop!
    Beau-ootiful Soo-oop!
Soo-oop of the e-e-evening,
    Beautiful, beautiful Soup!

Beautiful Soup! Who cares for fish,
Game, or any other dish?
Who would not give all else for two pennyworth
    only of beautiful Soup?
    Beau-ootiful Soup!
    Beau-ootiful Soup!
Soo-oop of the e-e-evening,
    Beautiful, beauti-FUL SOUP!

LEWIS CARROLL

The Duchess's Lullaby

Speak roughly to your little boy,
    And beat him when he sneezes;
He only does it to annoy,
    Because he knows it teases.
      Chorus: Wow! Wow! Wow!

I speak severely to my boy,
    I beat him when he sneezes;
For he can thoroughly enjoy
    The pepper when he pleases!
      Chorus: Wow! Wow! Wow!

LEWIS CARROLL

Atalanta in Camden-Town

Ay, 'twas here, on this spot,
    In that summer of yore,
Atalanta did not
    Vote my presence a bore,
Nor reply to my tenderest talk 'She had heard all that nonsense
    before.'

She'd the brooch I had bought
    And the necklace and sash on,
And her heart, as I thought,
    Was alive to my passion;
And she'd done up her hair in the style that the Empress had
    brought into fashion.

I had been to the play
    With my pearl of a Peri –
But, for all I could say,
    She declared she was weary,
That 'the place was so crowded and hot, and she couldn't abide that
    Dundreary'.

Then I thought 'Lucky boy!
    'Tis for you that she whimpers!'
And I noted with joy
    Those sensational simpers:
And I said 'This is scrumptious!' – a phrase I had learned from the
    Devonshire shrimpers.

And I vowed ''Twill be said
    I'm a fortunate fellow,
When the breakfast is spread,
    When the topers are mellow,
When the foam of the bride-cake is white, and the fierce orange-
    blossoms are yellow!'

O that languishing yawn!
    O those eloquent eyes!
I was drunk with the dawn
    Of a splendid surmise –
I was stung by a look, I was slain by a tear, by a tempest of sighs.

Then I whispered 'I see
    The sweet secret thou keepest,
And the yearning for ME
    That thou wistfully weepest!
And the question is "Licence or Banns?" though undoubtedly
    Banns are the cheapest.'

'Be my Hero,' said I
    'And let me be Leander!'

But I lost her reply –
   Something ending with 'gander' –
For the omnibus rattled so loud that no mortal could quite under-
   stand her.

LEWIS CARROLL

The Akond of Swat

Who or why, or which, or what,
         Is the Akond of SWAT?

Is he tall or short, or dark or fair?
Does he sit on a stool or a sofa or chair,
               or SQUAT,
         The Akond of Swat?

Is he wise or foolish, young or old?
Does he drink his soup and his coffee cold,
               or HOT,
         The Akond of Swat?

Does he sing or whistle, jabber or talk,
And when riding abroad does he gallop or walk,
               or TROT,
         The Akond of Swat?

Does he wear a turban, a fez, or a hat?
Does he sleep on a mattress, a bed, or a mat,
               or a COT,
         The Akond of Swat?

When he writes a copy in round-hand size,
Does he cross his T's and finish his I's
               with a DOT,
         The Akond of Swat?

Can he write a letter concisely clear
Without a speck or a smudge or smear
            or BLOT,
      The Akond of Swat?

Do his people like him extremely well?
Or do they, whenever they can, rebel,
            or PLOT
      At the Akond of Swat?

If he catches them then, either old or young,
Does he have them chopped in pieces or hung,
            or SHOT,
      The Akond of Swat?

Do his people prig in the lanes or park?
Or even at times, when days are dark,
            GAROTTE?
      O the Akond of Swat!

Does he study the wants of his own dominion?
Or doesn't he care for public opinion
            a JOT,
      The Akond of Swat?

To amuse his mind do his people show him
Pictures, or any one's last new poem,
            or WHAT,
      For the Akond of Swat?

At night if he suddenly screams and wakes,
Do they bring him only a few small cakes,
            or a LOT,
      For the Akond of Swat?

Does he live on turnips, tea, or tripe?
Does he like his shawl to be marked with a stripe,
      or a DOT,
    The Akond of Swat?

Does he like to lie on his back in a boat,
Like the lady who lived in that isle remote,
      SHALOTT,
    The Akond of Swat?

Is he quiet, or always making a fuss?
Is his steward a Swiss or a Swede or a Russ,
      or a SCOT,
    The Akond of Swat?

Does he like to sit by the calm blue wave?
Or to sleep and snore in a dark green cave,
      or a GROTT,
    The Akond of Swat?

Does he drink small beer from a silver jug?
Or a bowl? or a glass? or a cup? or a mug?
      or a POT,
    The Akond of Swat?

Does he beat his wife with a gold-topped pipe,
When she lets the gooseberries grow too ripe,
      or ROT,
    The Akond of Swat?

Does he wear a white tie when he dines with friends,
And tie it neat in a bow with ends,
      or a KNOT,
    The Akond of Swat?

Does he like new cream, and hate mince-pies?
When he looks at the sun does he wink his eyes,
                        or NOT,
            The Akond of Swat?

Does he teach his subjects to roast and bake?
Does he sail about on an inland lake,
                        in a YACHT,
            The Akond of Swat?

Some one, or nobody, knows, I wot,
Who or which or why or what
                Is the Akond of Swat!

                                    EDWARD LEAR

The Played-Out Humorist

Quixotic is his enterprise, and hopeless his adventure is,
    Who seeks for jocularities that haven't yet been said.
The world has joked incessantly for over fifteen centuries,
    And every joke that's possible has long ago been made.
I started as a humorist with lots of mental fizziness,
    But humour is a drug which it's the fashion to abuse;
For my stock-in-trade, my fixtures, and the goodwill of the
    business
No reasonable offer I am likely to refuse.
        And if anybody choose
        He may circulate the news
That no reasonable offer I'm likely to refuse.

Oh happy was that humorist – the first that made a pun at all –
    Who when a joke occurred to him, however poor and mean,
Was absolutely certain that it never had been done at all –
    How popular at dinners must that humorist have been!

Oh the days when some stepfather for a query held a handle out,
  The door-mat from the scraper, is it distant very far?
And when no one knew where Moses was when Aaron blew the
    candle out,
  And no one had discovered that a door could be a-jar!
    But your modern hearers are
    In their tastes particular,
  And they sneer if you inform them that a door can be a-jar!

In search of quip and quiddity, I've sat all day, alone, apart —
  And all that I could hit on as a problem was — to find
Analogy between a scrag of mutton and a Bony-part,
  Which offers slight employment to the speculative mind:
For you cannot call it very good, however great your charity —
  It's not the sort of humour that is greeted with a shout —
And I've come to the conclusion that my mine of jocularity,
  In present Anno Domini, is worked completely out!
    Though the notion you may scout,
    I can prove beyond a doubt
  That my mine of jocularity is utterly worked out!

                                        SIR W. S. GILBERT

A Lunatic's Love Song

O, know you the land where the cheese-tree grows,
And the unicorn spins on the end of his nose;
Where the sea-mew scowls on the circling bat,
And the elephant hunts in an opera hat?

'Tis there that I lie with my head in a pond,
And play with a valueless Tichborne bond;
'Tis there that I sip pure Horniman's tea
To the sound of the gong and the howling sea.

'Tis there that I revel in soapsuds and rum,
And wait till my creditors choose to come;
'Tis there that I dream of the days when I
Shall soar to the moon through the red-hot sky.

Then come, oh come to that happy land!
And don't forget your galvanic band;
We will play at cards in the lion's den,
And go to bed when the clock strikes ten.

ANON

The Rake's Progress

Born lorn,
Dad bad,
Nurse worse;
'Drat brat!'
School – Fool,
Work – shirk
Gal pal,
Splash cash,
Bets – debts,
Pop shop.
Nil – Till!
Boss – loss
Wired 'Fired!'
Scrub pub,
Drink – Brink –
Found Drowned.
'De Se';
Grief brief.

G. W. BRODRIBB

The Rondeau of the Knock

He took the knock! No more with jaunty air
He'll have the push that made the punter stare;
 No more in monkeys now odds on he'll lay
 And make the ever grumbling fielder gay.
One plunger more has had his little flare
And then came Monday when he couldn't square;
 Stripped of his plumes, a poor denuded J.,
   He took the knock!
Where is he now? Ah! Echo answers 'where?'

 Upon the turf he had his little day
 And when, stone-broke, he could no longer pay,
Leaving the ring to gnash its teeth and swear,
   He took the knock!

G. R. SIMS

Korf's Clock

Korf's clock is of a novel sort
In which two pairs of hands are used:
One pair points forwards as it ought,
The other backwards *à la Proust*.

When it says eight it's also four,
When it says nine it's also three;
A single glance and you no more
Need fear the ancient Enemy.

For with this wondrous clock you'll find
As, Janus-like, it turns about
(To such an end it was designed)
Time simply cancels itself out.

CHRISTIAN MORGENSTERN
(translated by R. F. C. HULL)

Palmström's Clock

But Palmström's has a 'higher' power,
Balanced as lightly as a flower.

Scorning a set pedestrian pace,
It keeps time with a certain grace

And will, in answer to a prayer,
  Go *en retard, en arrière*.

One hour, two hours, three hours indeed,
Sympathizing with our need!

Though clockwork in its outward part
It hides within — a tender heart.

CHRISTIAN MORGENSTERN
(translated by R. F. C. HULL)

The Official

Korf has been besieged by swarms
Of grim official-looking forms
Adjuring him to make reply
Who he is and what and why.

Where he resides, what his address is
And what profession he professes,
Where he was born (with day and date)
And whether he is celibate.

Why he had come into this town
And if he thought of settling down
And how much money he possessed
And what religion he thought best.

Contrariwise if he declined
To answer with an open mind
He'd be arrested without fail
And promptly taken off to jail!

Korf sent an answer mild and bland:
'Your letter of the 10th to hand.
The undersigned herewith presents
His most obsequious compliments,

But would apprise you of the fact
That, in the strict sense of the Act
As touching personal matters, he
Is a complete nonentity

And that, officially at least,
He much regrets not to exist.'
The High Official gasped – and read
With eyes fair bursting from his head.

CHRISTIAN MORGENSTERN
(translated by R. F. C. HULL)

Palmström Sculptor

Palmström shakes up his bed with so much feeling
That all his room looks like a Sistine ceiling:
Peopled with gods, and giants and splendid women.

He lunges back and forth with wild invective,
Swinging his lantern o'er the mangled linen
To get his visions into true perspective.

And in the changing play of lights and shadows
He sees madonnas, cherubs and mulattos,
Athletes with snakes and Venuses in foam.

And dreams: were this but real and not mere feather,
'Twould shame the Golden Age and altogether
Eclipse the gloried pomps of Greece and Rome!

CHRISTIAN MORGENSTERN
(translated by R. F. C. HULL)

The Impossible Fact

Professor Palmström, it appears,
Already getting on in years,
Stood at a busy terminus
And got run over by a bus.

'How was it,' he exclaimed anon
And resolutely living on,
'Possible that such a fall
Should ever have occurred at all?

Cannot one claim some compensation
For faulty traffic regulation?
Are cars by order of police
Allowed to do just what they please?

Or is it not prohibited
To turn live people into dead?
And finally, in such a crowd,
Should *any* traffic be allowed?'

Enveloped in wet towels at home
He scans a monstrous legal tome
Till all at once the thing is clear:
No cars should use that thoroughfare!

And so he comes to the conclusion:
The whole affair was an illusion.
'For look,' he cries triumphantly,
'What's not permitted CANNOT be!'

CHRISTIAN MORGENSTERN
(translated by R. F. C. HULL)

The Two Bottles

Two bottles stood upon a bin.
The one was fat, the other thin.
Fain would they taste of married bliss,
But who'll give them advice on this?

And with their suffering double-eye
They gaze into the empty sky.
But no one leaves his heavenly station
To grant the poor dears copulation.

CHRISTIAN MORGENSTERN
(translated by R. F. C. HULL)

The Handkerchief Ghost

There is a ghost
That eats handkerchiefs;
It keeps you company
On all your travels, and
Eats your handkerchiefs
Out of your trunk, your
Bed, your washstand,
Like a bird eating
Out of your hand, – not
All of them and not
All at one go. With

Eighteen handkerchiefs
You set out, a proud mariner,
On the seas of the Unknown;
With eight or perhaps
Seven you come back, the
Despair of the housewife.

CHRISTIAN MORGENSTERN
(translated by R. F. C. HULL)

The Fence

There was a fence with spaces you
Could look through if you wanted to.

An architect who saw this thing
Stood there one summer evening,

Took out the spaces with great care
And built a castle in the air.

The fence was utterly dumbfounded:
Each post stood there with nothing round it.

A sight most terrible to see.
(They charged it with indecency.)

The architect then ran away
To Afric- or Americ-ay.

CHRISTIAN MORGENSTERN
(translated by R. F. C. HULL)

The Sandwich Paper

There was a Sandwich paper which
Mysteriously began to itch.

And in its fear, although till now
It had no thought of thinking – how

Could it indeed, having no head
Worth mentioning – now (from fear, I said)

Began, commenced (you'll hardly guess)
To feel the dawn of consciousness,

To think, to cogitate, to be,
Acquire a personality

Which, be it noted, was not sent
By chance out of the firmament,

But rose out of an earthly plane,
The product of an actual brain,

Whose substance (albumen and glue)
Found in the sandwich paper (through

A permutation, or a sort
Of evolutionary 'sport')

In this same sandwich paper found
Form, content, happy breeding-ground.

Taking advantage of this fact
The paper now resolved to act,

To live, to love, to walk, to try
To flutter like a butterfly ...

To crawl at first and then to rise
On wings before our wondering eyes,

Then back and forth and to and fro
As all such heavenly creatures go

Who with the zephyrs dip and play
High o'er our hapless human clay!

But O my friends, give ear, give heed!
A Sparrow, fat and full of greed

Espies it, and with tooth and nail
(How end this bitter moral tale!)

With tooth and nail and nail and tooth
(But truth will out, the dreadful Truth!)

(My pen shakes and the ink grows pale!)
Gets ready, sharpening tooth and nail . . .

Stop, stop! Enough! Fate will not yield!
The Sandwich paper's doom is sealed!

The vile bird in one horrid spasm
Devoured this priceless protoplasm.

CHRISTIAN MORGENSTERN
(translated by R. F. C. HULL)

The Experiment

Once for experiment I bought
A needle of the better sort.

And furthermore a camel, old
Though one must add, extremely bold.

A rich man too was there with me
Together with his L.S.D.

The rich man, I need hardly tell,
Went up to Heaven and rang the bell.

Thereat spake Peter: 'It stands writ
That any camel, strong and fit

Shall pass the needle's eye before
You put a foot across this door!'

Not doubting God's words in the least
I reassured the valiant beast

Holding behind the needle's eye
A toothsome slice of cherry pie!

And on my oath, the beast went through
– Though creaking cruelly, it is true.

The rich man, who could only blink,
Turned round and muttered: 'Strike me pink!'

CHRISTIAN MORGENSTERN
(translated by R. F. C. HULL)

Ballade of Modified Regrets

Shooting one day with other people in
A wood called Archers on the Upper Clyde,
I caught a certain Scotchman on the shin
From aiming rather badly down the ride.
It wounded him – not only in his pride –
And ever since he goes a trifle lame:
And when I meet him now I run and hide.
I fear that I was more or less to blame.

In Norfolk, in the ancient town of Lynn,
I brought up sharply, on a racing tide,
A lovely little yawl, which to begin
With wasn't mine: that cannot be denied.
A man had lent it me. And, as I tried
To pick up moorings and make fast the same,
I caught a post, which smashed her starboard side.
I fear that I was more or less to blame.

Another time, when I was keen to win
A friend a by-election, I applied
To both the Central Offices for tin,
And by judicious hints of trouble guyed
Them both into disbursing loose and wide.
Well. Politics is a disgusting game,
But still – how monumentally I lied!
I fear that I was more or less to blame.

ENVOI

Prince, when you caught that little butter-slide
Against the Palace, what a smack you came!
Laugh? Bless your soul! I thought I should have died.
. . . I fear that I was more or less to blame.

HILAIRE BELLOC

Scotch Rhapsody

'Do not take a bath in Jordan,
                          Gordon,
On the holy Sabbath, on the peaceful day!'
Said the huntsman, playing on his old bagpipe,
Boring to death the pheasant and the snipe –
Boring the ptarmigan and grouse for fun –
Boring them worse than a nine-bore gun.

Till the flaxen leaves where the prunes are ripe,
Hear the tartan wind a-droning in the pipe,
And they heard McPherson say:
'Where do the waves go? What hotels
Hide their bustles and their gay ombrelles?
And would there be room? – Would there be *room?*
    Would there be room for me?'
There is a hotel at Ostend
Cold as the wind, without an end,
Haunted by ghostly poor relations
Of Bostonian conversations
(Bagpipes rotting through the walls.)
And there the pearl-ropes fall like shawls
With a noise like marine waterfalls.
And 'Another little drink wouldn't do us any harm'
Pierces through the Sabbatical calm.
And that is the place for me!
So do not take a bath in Jordan, Gordon,
On the holy Sabbath on the peaceful day –
Or you'll never go to heaven, Gordon McPherson,
And speaking purely as a private person
That is the place – *that* is the place – that is the *place* for me!

DAME EDITH SITWELL

Mrs Busk

On dull mornings
    When the sun was bolstered,
        Buried in feathers,
It yet shone whitely in the fish-market,
    Playing on the scaly surfaces of quays,
Among the glistening curves and planes of iridescent mounds.
Here, as on a stone raft between the seas,
        The fish-wives,
        Armed with knives,

Called to each other over damp, slimy stalls
      With thick briny laughter.
Here Mrs Busk, a mountain in oilskin
      With a creased tarpaulin face,
      Bought her wares,
  Squeezing, testing, prodding with appraising thumb and finger.

Later, in a voice like a loving cat,
She cried '*Fish*' over every street
Her howl, without pity, seemed to govern the town,
Making all men equal.
Inhuman, it floated in at fashionable windows
And at those that gaped like caves,
Over the rain-grey slates and the red-ribbed roofs,
Oracular, like that of a prophetess foretelling doom universal:
  '*Fresh Whiting, Fine Whiting!*
     Fresh Codfish, Fine Codfish!'

                    SIR OSBERT SITWELL

Quote Buns by Great Men Quote

         one of the most
         pathetic things i
         have seen recently
         was an intoxicated person
         trying to fall
         down a moving stairway
         it was the escalator at
         the thirty fourth street
         side of the
         pennsylvania station
         he could not fall down as
         fast as it
         carried him up again but
         he was game he kept on

trying he was
stubborn about it
evidently it was a part of
his tradition habit and
he did not intend to
be defeated this time i
watched him for an hour
and moved sadly away thinking
how much sorrow
drink is responsible for the
buns by great men
reached and kept
are not attained
by sudden flight but they
while their companions slept
were falling upwards
through the night

                         archy

                       DON MARQUIS

No Doctors Today, Thank You

They tell me that euphoria is the feeling of feeling wonderful; well,
    today I feel euphorian,
Today I have the agility of a Greek God and the appetite of a
    Victorian,
Yes, today I may even go forth without my galoshes;
Today I am a swashbuckler, would anybody like me to buckle my
    swashes?
This is my euphorian day.
I will ring welkins and before anybody answers I will run away.
I will tame me a caribou
And bedeck it with marabou.
I will pen me my memoirs.
Ah, youth, youth! What euphorian days them was!

I wasn't much of a hand for the boudoirs,
I was generally to be found where the food was.
Does anybody want any flotsam?
I've gotsam.
Does anybody want any jetsam?
I can getsam.
I can play 'Chopsticks' on the Wurlitzer,
I can speak Portuguese like a Berlitzer.
I can don or doff my shoes without tying or untying the laces
      because I am wearing moccasins,
And I practically know the difference between serums and anti-
      toccasins.
Kind people, don't think me purse-proud, don't set me down as
      vainglorious,
I'm just a little euphorious.

OGDEN NASH

Ask Daddy, He Won't Know

Now that they've abolished chrome work
I'd like to call their attention to home work.
Here it is only three decades since my scholarship was famous,
And I'm an ignoramus.
I cannot think which goes sideways and which goes up and down,
      a parallel or a meridian,
Nor do I know the name of him who first transplanted the Bible
      into Indian, I see him only as an enterprising colonial
      Gideon.
I have difficulty with dates,
To say nothing of the annual rainfall of the Southern Central
      States,
And the only way I can distinguish proper from improper fractions
Is by their actions.
Naturally the correct answers are just back of the tip of my tongue,

But try to explain that to your young.
I am overwhelmed by their erudite banter,
I am in no condition to differentiate between Tamerlane and Tam
    o' Shanter.
I reel, I sway, I am utterly exhausted;
Should you ask me when Chicago was founded I could only reply
    I didn't know it was losted.

OGDEN NASH

Peekaboo, I almost See You

Middle-aged life is merry, and I love to lead it,
But there comes a day when your eyes are all right, but your arm
    isn't long enough to hold the telephone book where you
    can read it,
And your friends get jocular, so you go to the oculist,
And of all your friends he is the joculist,
So over his facetiousness let us skim,
Only noting that he has been waiting for you ever since you said
    Good Evening to his grandfather clock under the impres-
    sion that it was him.
And you look at his chart and it says SHRDLU QWERTYOP, and
    you say Well, why SHRDNTLU QWERTYOP? and he says
    one set of glasses won't do.
You need two,
One for reading Erle Stanley Gardner's Perry Mason and Keats's
    'Endymion' with,
And the other for walking around without saying Hallo to strange
    wymion with.
So you spend your time taking off your seeing glasses to put on
    your reading glasses, and then remembering that your
    reading glasses are upstairs or in the car,

And then you can't find your seeing glasses again because without
    them you can't see where they are.
Enough of such mishaps, they would try the patience of an ox,
I prefer to forget both pairs of glasses and pass my declining years
    saluting strange women and grandfather clocks.

OGDEN NASH

Lament

'I was never chairman of the company, so far as I know' — *Old Bailey Remark*

    I heard a voice complain in Fenchurch Street,
    Very bitterly it grieved, saying:

1

I wish I knew if I was chairman of this company,
It would make a lot of difference at conferences:
Gorgeous conferences we have, simply gorgeous,
Finest in the City, I imagine.
I am always in the top chair, but the boys will never let on if I'm
    chairman or not.

2

Sometimes after a jolly fine conference I say: 'Boys, that was a fine
    conference, let's have another.'
Then we have another, right on the spot.
I often slip in a word, as if joking, such as 'Looks to me as if I'm
    chairman of this company', but nobody ever takes it up.
Often when I'm signing things or shouting into my dictaphone
    (you ought to see my dictaphone) or maybe ringing
    through to main office and firing somebody, I wish one of
    the boys would just say: 'Look at old Fishy — he's chair-
    man, you know.'
Nobody ever does.

3

For Heaven's sake, why can't they be frank with me one way or
    another?
If they'd just say: 'All right, old boy, you're chairman', I could do
    a lot of things I've always wanted to do.
Such as swinging a big merger,
Or correlating overhead with saturation-point,
Or getting a whole lot of people, say twenty or thirty, on the mat
    at once and raking them with merciless eyes and saying:
    'You're out!'
I'd get a chairman's portion on the *Southern Belle* too.
Dear Heaven, why can't they tell me?

D. B. WYNDHAM LEWIS

Posy

FOR A TALL NOISY GIRL HEARD AT A BOTTLE PARTY, 3.30 A.M.

Sweetheart, in all your girlish charm you are
Like laughter at a West End Cinema
When lightning wisecracks flash and spurt and throng:
Too loud, my Love; too late; and far too long.

D. B. WYNDHAM LEWIS

There's Money in Mother and Father

The lamp burns long in the cottage,
    The light shines late in the shop,
Their beams disclosing the writers composing
    Memories of Mom and Pop.

    Oh don't write a book about Father!
        Don't write a book about Dad!
    Better not bother to tell how Father
        Went so amusingly mad.

Better pass over the evening
   Father got locked in the zoo —
For your infant son has possibly begun
   A funny little book about you.

The author broods in his study,
   The housewife dreams in her flat:
Since Mommer and Popper were most improper,
   There ought to be a book in that.

But don't write a book about Mother!
   Don't write a book about Mum!
We all know Mumsy was vague and clumsy,
   Dithering, drunken and dumb.
There may be money in Mother,
   And possibly a movie, too —
But some little mite is learning how to write
   To write a little book about you.

MORRIS BISHOP

I hear America Singing, Credit Lines[1]

The poets go hippety-hoppety
   To the office to draw their pay;
'Proputty, proputty, proputty' —
   That's what I 'ears 'em say.[2]

And there the office factotum
   Watches o'er every phrase,
And if anyone wants to quote 'em,
   By golly, he pays and pays.[3]

1. All rights reserved, including the right to reproduce anything or portions thereof, by the author and publisher.

2. By permission of the heirs of Alfred, Lord Tennyson, Aldworth, Blackdown above Haslemere, Surrey, England.

3. From *The Woman Who Pays*, by Will D. Cobb, music by Gus Edwards. By permission of the publishers, Edward B. Marks Music Corporation.

A fellow who writes or edits
    And includes a fragment of song
Had better give proper credits
    Or Ascap will do him wrong.[4]

When you read some novelist's hit, mark
    That no one sings or recites
A line unless Marks or Witmark
    Has ceded the copyrights.

Oh, I think it is frightfully funny
    That our words are restricted thus,
But put them all together they spell *money*,
    A name that means the world to us.[5]

                                    MORRIS BISHOP

Bruno Pim

I often think of Bruno Pim
And wonder what's become of him;
He always was evolving schemes
Far wilder than your wildest dreams,
And once he lit with phosphorus
A lighthouse on the Bosporus.

Soon afterwards they said that he
Was harnessing the bumble-bee
And utilizing bamboo-shoots
To make elastic-sided boots.
Then he ('twas hardly rational)
Rode yaks in the Grand National.

---

4. From *Frankie and Johnny*, author unknown. A reserve fund has been established to pay eventual claims.

5. From *Mother*, words by Howard Johnson and music by T. Morse.   By permission of the publishers, Leo Feist Inc.

Dispirited he made at home
A giant silent metronome
And next was seen in New Orleans
Outdistancing some runner beans.
He then wrote his biography
Entitled: 'Pim's Cosmography'.

This work, twelve volumes, did not sell
Alas, particularly well
And so, disgruntled, he then planned
To make explosives out of sand.
Rumour has it, he succeeded,
Reached the moon quite unimpeded.

                                                    ALAN CRICK

A Chance Meeting

I met such a singular man today,
His appearance seems worthy of note;
He was wearing some spurs in the usual way
And a tangerine overcoat.

But that was not all, for he wore a silk hat
Around which was hanging some lace,
And between this fine fringe and his fluffy cravat
You might possibly make out his face.

I was not so much struck by this elegant dress
As his eager pursuit of a game;
He was playing himself at some strenuous chess
Which he wheeled on a wickerwork frame.

He was, so it seemed to me, pressed for time,
For he glanced now and then at a clock

With triangular dial and a flat-toned chime
Which he drew from an old puce sock.

At regular intervals he'd indulge
In a pinch from a ladle of snuff,
And his normally cavernous cheeks would bulge
As he pensively chewed the stuff.

But time was up and he had to go,
So he packed up his chattels in sieves,
Why and whither he went I should like to know —
And I'm wondering where he lives?

ALAN CRICK

Crime and Punishment

I will not dance upon my ears,
I find it hurts my head;
Nor will I sleep on chandeliers
For I prefer my bed.

I cannot, will not live on oats
Nor eat those two-inch nails
While I am forced to feed my goats
On aromatic quails.

I cannot for the life of me
Grow toadstools on my hat —
And as for mouse-traps in my tea
My patience ends at that.

O why must you torment me so
And cause me all this pain?
Cease! and I promise that I will
Not try to sing again.

ALAN CRICK

Diplomatic Catechism

Q. Who engineered the Trans-Ugandian Disruption?
Who deposited the cobras in the Minister's bed?
Was it you who arranged the advantageous exit
From the Bulgarian Mint? Come, was it you?
And if not, who?

A. O, really, gentlemen,
I did none of these things, not one; when each one happened
I was somewhere else; yes, once with a red-haired dancer,
Once chasing boars in the tall Carpathian Mountains,
And once I was immersed in my model trains.

Q. *Someone* removed that agent from his head,
Someone used the syringe on those poisoned grapes,
Someone endeavoured to retire with the map-maker's wife,
Someone has laboured, laboured. Come, was it you?
And if not, who?

A. Well, really, gentlemen,
I could speak to my confrères, who must here be nameless,
I could look into my records, or even look over my diary.
Have you read my little book on my Kurdish exploits?
The clue may well be there. My memory's rather musty.

Q. Who slew the wicker-works chap and provoked a scandal?
Who derailed the Trans-Time Express and stole the Queen?
Who put up the anti-aircraft on the Acropolis
And shot down Icarus? Come, was it you,
And if not, who?

A. O, dear, O, dear,
Really, you know, gentlemen, O, yes, really, you know,
You can't accuse me without substantiation.

I'm a peaceful, home-keeping man, I work in my garden,
Love my good wife, like pie, look well for my age,
Keep a strict vegetable diet, smoke no pipe.
If I have, shall we say, a quiet passion for intrigue,
It's merely a whim, and hardly of prime importance.
That which you see there bleeding is my heart.
That which you smell there burning is my zeal.
Good day, good day, good day.

HARRY BROWN

Problem Child

How *shall* I deal with Roger,
                    Mrs Prodger?
I've never yet been able
To sit him at a table
And make him paint a label
For the salmon in the kindergarten shop.
            But he's full of animation
            When I mention a dictation,
                    And he never wants a spelling-test to stop.
I've encouraged self-expression
And intentional digression
But I think I'll have to let the system drop.
            For the normal child, like Roger,
            Is a *do*-er, not a dodger,
And your methods, Mrs Prodger, are a flop.

How *shall* I deal with Roger,
                    Mrs Prodger?
I've had projects on the fairies,
On markets, shops and dairies;
I've had projects on the *prairies*,
But the little fellow doesn't want to play:
            Instead he has a yearning

For unreasonable learning,
And wants to do Arithmetic all day.
He shows a strong proclivity
For purposeless activity,
And doesn't want experience in clay.
So I rather think that Roger
Is a *do*-er, not a dodger,
And how *would* you deal with Roger, can you say?

J. E. FAULKS

On the Twelfth Day of Christmas I Screamed

(A LETTER FROM HIS GIRL TO A G.I. IN TOKYO)

Now April's here, what ever can I do
With those fantastic gifts I got from you?
Spring's in the air, but, honey, life is hard:
The three French hens are picking in the yard,
And the turtledove, the turtledove
(One of them died) –
Ah, love, my own true love, you have denied
Me nothing the mails or the express could bring.
But look: we're into spring;
The calling birds are calling, calling;
The pear tree's leaves are slowly falling;
I sit here with those cackling geese
And never know a moment's peace.
My memories are mixed and hazy,
The drumming drummers drive me crazy,
The milking maids enjoy canasta,
The lords are leaping ever faster,
The pipers – God in Heaven knows
I've more than had enough of those.

My love, you do such wondrous things
(Who else would think of *five* gold rings?)

I know you send me all you can
Of spoils of occupied Japan,
But you remain on alien shore
And waiting here is such a bore.
My love, the lively lords are leaping:
Some things will not improve with keeping.

Now April's here, the weary days go by;
I watch that wretched dove attempt to fly;
The partridge smells; the geese are getting hoarse;
My diction's growing positively coarse.
You must forgive my gestures of rejection –
I'm crazed with all your tokens of affection.
Enough's enough; next time be less romantic
And don't send gifts that drive a lady frantic.
Send me a postcard with a pretty view
And I shall look at it and think of you.

DAVID DAICHES

Anatomy of the Emotions

These warning words I write as Muses bid me:
Be brave in *heart* and *head* like Philip Sidney
And other gallant worthies of that *kidney*.

In fighting – no retreating once you're in.
Just stick it out, whether you lose or win:
You must have *guts* to take it on the *chin*.

The man who cannot *stomach* fights – refuses
Combats which his alert opponent chooses –
Has lost his *ear* for praises by the Muses.

(I knew a fellow once who stood and shivered
In face of any risk. His *limbs* all quivered.
It seems to me that he was lily-*livered*.)

If by some secret guilt you are oppressed,
Go cough it up and get it off your *chest* –
Make a clean *breast* is best, the crime confessed.

Kind *hearts* are more than coronets; the charm
Of clean *hands* counteracts an itchy *palm*.
(But too much *lip* can do a fellow harm.)

From older literature it can be seen
That men were once much troubled by the *spleen*:
It chilled the *blood* with dismal gloom, I ween,

A most unhappy fate. Nor is this all:
A man could be affected by his *gall*,
Which made his *bowels* of compassion small.

P'raps I should add that bowels of compassion
(Well known in Bible times) are out of fashion.

DAVID DAICHES

La Donna È Perpetuum Mobile

Now Mrs Eberle early had been told
That speech, not silence, was authentic gold:
In conversation there must be no pause
When guests are present, even one's in-laws;
Especially with strangers, one must chatter
Continuously – on whatever matter;
And as for thoughts, there never need be any
Conceivably worth anybody's penny.

I meet the lady often. . . . Rat-tat-tat!
Her tongue is loosed before I tip my hat;
After a burst of saturation talk,
My spirit battered, I resume my walk.

Met at a party, she'll rush up with questions,
Answer herself with whirlwinds of suggestions.
Move on to others, talking – there she is,
Now here, now there, a self-replying quiz.

Mention of a place (say, India) where you've been;
She tells of books she's read, of plays she's seen,
All about India, and a man she knew
Who lived a hermit's life in Timbuktu –
Oh, that's not India! But there was a swami,
Heavenly-looking, though a little balmy.
'I'd love to see Iran,' she says. 'Would you?'
She recalls the Persian show in London, too.
And that reminds her of 'My Persian Rose',
Sung when she was a child – here's how it goes!
She'd *love* to see the Taj Mahal, but guesses
Most places in the East are horrid messes;
Even in peacetime, food in Asia's bad,
But she loves curry. Do I? Yes, She's glad.

And so it goes and goes, and flows and flows –
A stream, as though she were a verbal hose,
Of things she's heard, of things she thinks she knows.
Could I but choke her, cut her head off clean,
I mean – well, really, that's *just* what I mean.

IRWIN EDMAN

Ballad of Domestic Calamity

('Our postillion has been struck by lightning' is one of the 'useful Common Phrases' appearing in a Dutch manual on the speaking of English)

To every man upon this earthly ball
    Misfortune comes, and not a soul is free;
It claims alike the master and the thrall,
    The hungry plumber and the proud J.P.;

But never did the eye of mortal see
A tragedy more sudden and more frightening
 Than what has happened to my wife and me:
Look! our postillion has been struck by lightning.

We had attained the topmost branch of all
 In our slow progress up the social tree;
We had quite recently acquired the Hall,
 Our menial staff had swelled to twenty-three;
 And now, in this blest year of Jubilee,
When all seemed fair and every hope was brightening,
 When Lady Parks had asked us out to tea,
Our – postillion has been struck by lightning.

Not singly do terrestrial troubles fall:
 Our second groom has water on the knee;
The seventh footman thinks he is ST PAUL,
 The butler and the parlourmaid agree;
 The gardener's boy is out upon the spree,
The cook is tight; the scullery-maid is tightening,
 The under-boots has failed his Pass Degree,
And our postillion has been struck by lightning.

ENVOI

Prince, we intended for a moderate fee
 To come and drown you in a pail of whitening;
But life is life, and it was not to be,
 For our postillion has been struck by lightning.

         M. H. LONGSON

Ballade to my Psycho-Analyst

I am concerned because my mind
 Contains no subterranean lair;

Nothing abysmal lurks behind
  My neatly brushed and parted hair;
  No hidden conflict anywhere,
And no neurosis worth the name:
  This has reduced me to despair:
I go about in guilt and shame.

My dreams are the pedestrian kind,
  And come with symbols sparse and bare,
As unexcited and refined
  As ever faced a censor's stare.
  They stand before the censor's chair
And giggle as he calls their name,
  'But we have nothing to declare'.
I go about in guilt and shame.

My deep unconscious was designed
  To function with conditioned air,
And when you lift the lid you find
  No evil brew fermenting there;
  Plenty of good plain wholesome fare –
Sardines in tins and potted game –
  But nothing high and nothing rare.
I go about in guilt and shame.

ENVOI

Prince, you descend my spiral stair:
  No shadows flee your candle flame:
Where is the foetal matter? Where?
  I go about in guilt and shame.

KENNETH LILLINGTON

Sartorial Solecism

Poor Uncle Joe
Can't help his face,
But what I wished to know
Was why he must us all disgrace
By wearing a thing so out of place
As a bowler-hat for sailing!

Said Auntie Flo:
'It may not be
Quite the thing to wear at sea,
But look how well it softens the blow
When the boom swings over on Uncle Joe!
Besides, it's grand for bailing.'

R. E. C. STRINGER

Park Concert

Astounding the bucolic grass,
The bandsmen sweat in golds and reds
And put their zeal into the brass.
A glorious flustered major heads

Their sort of stationary charge.
Their lips are pursed, their cheeks get pink;
The instruments are very large
Through which they render Humperdinck.

The sailors and the parlourmaids
Both vote the music jolly good,
But do not worry if it fades
As they stroll deeper in the wood,

Where twenty French horns wouldn't stir
A leaf. The intrepid band try not
To mind the applause (as though it were
A testing fusilade of shot),

Polish their mouthpieces and cough,
Then throw their shoulders back to play
A Pomeranian march. They're off!
And Sousa scares the tits away.

JAMES MICHIE

To the Inevitable Optimist

These days I feel like a man on a cold dawn deck,
  With Mr Masefield's wind like a whetted knife
Sliding between my muffler and my neck
  And cutting short my expectation of life.
At night in bed, I feel a trifle stronger –
Don't tell me that the days are getting longer.

DONALD MATTAM

Oh kittens, in our hours of ease
Uncertain toys and full of fleas,
When pain and anguish hang o'er men,
We turn you into sausage then.

ANON.

DOUBTFUL TALES

The Precise Tailor

A tailor, thought a man of upright dealing –
True, but for lying; honest, but for stealing –
Did fall one day extremely sick by chance,
And on the sudden was in wond'rous trance;
The fiends of hell, must'ring in fearful manner,
Of sundry-colour'd silks display'd a banner
Which he had stolen, and wish'd, as they did tell,
That he might find it all one day in hell.
The man, affrighted with this apparition,
Upon recov'ry grew a great precision:
He bought a Bible of the best translation,
And in his life he show'd great reformation;
He walked mannerly, he talk'd meekly,
He heard three lectures and two sermons weekly;
He vow'd to shun all company unruly,
And in his speech he used no oath but truly;
And zealously to keep the Sabbath's rest,
His meat for that day on the eve was drest;
And lest the custom which he had to steal
Might cause him sometimes to forget his zeal,
He gave his journeyman a special charge,
That if the stuff, allowance being large,
He found his fingers were to filch inclined,
Bid him to have the banner in his mind.
This done (I scant can tell the rest for laughter!)
A captain of a ship came three days after,
And brought three yards of velvet and three-quarters
To make Venetians down below the garters.
He, that precisely knew how much was enough,
Soon slipt aside three quarters of the stuff;
His man, espying it, said in derision:
'Master, remember how you saw the vision!'
'Peace, knave!' quoth he, 'I did not see one rag
Of such a colour'd silk in all the flag.'

SIR JOHN HARINGTON

Wednesbury Cocking

At Wednesbury there was a cocking,
    A match between Newton and Scroggins;
The colliers and nailers left work,
    And all to old Spittle's went jogging.
To see this noble sport,
    Many noblemen resorted;
And though they'd but little money,
    Yet that little they freely sported.

There was Jeffery and Colborn from Hampton,
    And Dusty from Bilston was there;
Flummery he came from Darlaston,
    And he was as rude as a bear.
There was old Will from Walsall,
    And Smacker from Westbromwich come;
Blind Robin he come from Rowley,
    And staggering he went home.

Ralph Moody came hobbling along,
    As though he some cripple was mocking,
To join in the blackguard throng,
    That met at Wednesbury cocking.
He borrowed a trifle of Doll,
    To back old Taverner's grey;
He laid fourpence-halfpenny to fourpence,
    He lost and went broken away.

But soon he returned to the pit,
    For he'd borrowed a trifle more money,
And ventured another large bet,
    Along with blobbermouth Coney.
When Coney demanded his money,
    As is usual on all such occasions,

He cried, 'Rot thee, if thee don't hold thy rattle,
   I'll pay thee as Paul paid the Ephasians.'

The morning's sport being over,
   Old Spittle a dinner proclaimed,
Each man he should dine for a groat,
   If he grumbled he ought to be maimed,
For there was plenty of beef,
   But Spittle he swore by his troth,
That never a man he should dine
   Till he ate his noggin of broth.

The beef it was old and tough,
   Off a bull that was baited to death,
Barney Hyde got a lump in his throat,
   That had like to have stopped his breath,
The company all fell into confusion,
   At seeing poor Barney Hyde choke;
So they took him into the kitchen,
   And held him over the smoke.

They held him so close to the fire,
   He frizzled just like a beef-steak,
They then threw him down on the floor,
   Which had like to have broken his neck.
One gave him a kick in the stomach,
   Another a kick on the brow,
His wife said, 'Throw him into the stable,
   And he'll be better just now.'

Then they all returned to the pit,
   And the fighting went forward again;
Six battles were fought on each side,
   And the next was to decide the main.
For they were two famous cocks
   As ever this country bred,

Scroggins's a dark winged black,
    And Newton's a shift winged red.

The conflict was hard on both sides,
    Till Brassy's black winged was choked;
The colliers were tarnationally vexed,
    And the nailers were sorely provoked.
Peter Stevens he swore a great oath,
    That Scroggins had played his cock foul;
Scroggins gave him a kick on the head,
And cried, 'Fiend fly off with thy soul.'

The company then fell in discord,
    A bold, bold fight did ensue;
Bite, bludgeon and bruise was the word,
    Till the Walsall men all were subdued.
Ralph Moody bit off a man's nose,
    And wished that he could have him slain,
So they trampled both cocks to death,
    And they made a draw of the main.

The cock-pit was near to the church,
    An ornament unto the town;
On one side an old coal pit,
    The other well gorsed around.
Peter Hadley peeped through the gorse,
    In order to see them fight;
Spittle jobbed out his eye with a fork,
    And said, 'Rot thee, it served thee right.'

Some people may think this strange,
    Who Wednesbury never knew;
But those who have ever been there,
    Will not have the least doubt it's true;
For they are as savage by nature,
    And guilty of deeds the most shocking;

Jack Baker whacked his own father,
And thus ended Wednesbury cocking.

ANON.

The Knight and the Lady

A DOMESTIC LEGEND OF THE REIGN OF QUEEN ANNE

The Lady Jane was tall and slim,
    The Lady Jane was fair,
And Sir Thomas, her Lord, was stout of limb,
But his cough was short, and his eyes were dim,
And he wore green 'specs', with a tortoiseshell rim,
And his hat was remarkably broad in the brim
And she was uncommonly fond of him, –
    And they were a loving pair! –
    And the name and the fame
    Of the Knight and his Dame,
Were ev'rywhere hail'd with the loudest acclaim;
And wherever they went, or wherever they came,
    Far and wide, The people cried,
'Huzzah! for the Lord of this noble domain, –
Huzzah! Huzzah! Huzzah! – once again! –
    Encore! – Encore! – One cheer more!
– All sorts of pleasure, and no sort of pain
    To Sir Thomas the Good, and the Fair Lady Jane!!'

Now Sir Thomas the Good, Be it well understood,
Was a man of a very contemplative mood, –
He would pore by the hour, O'er a weed or a flower,
Or the slugs that come crawling out of a shower;
Black-beetles, and Bumble-bees, – Blue-bottle flies,
And Moths were of no small account in his eyes;
An 'Industrious Flea' he'd by no means despise,
While an 'Old Daddy-long-legs', whose 'long legs' and thighs
Pass'd the common in shape, or in colour, or size,

He was wont to consider an absolute prize,
Nay a hornet or wasp he could scarce 'keep his paws off' – he
    Gave up, in short, Both business and sport,
And abandon'd himself, *tout entier*, to Philosophy.

Now, as Lady Jane was tall and slim,
    And Lady Jane was fair,
And a good many years the junior of him, –
    And as he, All agree,
    Look'd less like her *Mari*,
As he walk'd by her side, than her *Père*,[1]
There are some might be found entertaining a notion
That such an entire, and exclusive devotion
To that part of science, folks style Entomology,
    Was a positive shame, And, to such a fair Dame,
Really demanded some sort of apology:
    – No doubt it *would* vex One half of the sex
To see their own husband in horrid green 'specs',
Instead of enjoying a sociable chat,
Still poking his nose into this and to that,
    At a gnat, or a bat, or a cat, or a rat,
    Or great ugly things, All legs and wings,
With nasty long tails arm'd with nasty, long stings;
And they'd join such a log of a spouse to condemn,
    – One eternally thinking, And blinking and winking
At grubs, – when he ought to be winking at them –
    But no! – oh no! 'Twas by no means so
With the Lady Jane Ingoldsby – she, far discreeter,
And, having a temper more even and sweeter,
    Would never object to *Her* spouse, in respect to
    His poking and peeping After 'things creeping':
Much less be still keeping lamenting, and weeping,
Or scolding at what she perceived him so deep in.

1.   My friend, Mr Hood,
            In his comical mood,
  Would have probably styled the good Knight and his Lady –
Him 'Stern-old and Hopkins', and her 'Tête and Braidy.'

Tout au contraire, No lady so fair
Was e'er known to wear more contented an air;
And, let who would call, – every day she was there,
Propounding receipts for some delicate fare,
Some toothsome conserve, of quince, apple, or pear,
Or distilling strong waters, – or potting a hare, –
Or counting her spoons and her crockery-ware;
Or else, her tambour-frame before her, with care
Embroidering a stool or a back for a chair,
With needle-work roses, most cunning and rare,
Enough to make less gifted visitors stare,
    And declare, where'er
    They had been, that, 'they ne'er
In their lives had seen aught that at all could compare
With dear Lady Jane's housewifery' – that they would swear.

Nay more; don't suppose With such doings as those
This account of her merits must come to a close;
No; – Examine her conduct more closely, you'll find
She by no means neglected improving her mind;
For there, all the while, with air quite bewitching,
She sat herring-boning, tambouring, or stitching,
Or having an eye to affairs of the kitchen.
    Close by her side, Sat her kinsman, MacBride,
Her cousin, fourteen-times removed, – as you'll see
If you look at the Ingoldsby family tree,
In 'Burke's Commoners', vol. xx, page 53.
    All the papers I've read agree, Too, with the pedigree,
Where, among the collateral branches, appears
'Captain Dugald MacBride, Royal Scots Fusileers';
And I doubt if you'd find in the whole of his clan
A more highly-intelligent, worthy young man; –
    And there he'd be sitting, While she was a-knitting,
Or hemming, or stitching, or darning and fitting,
Or putting a 'gore', or a 'gusset', or 'bit' in,

Reading aloud, with a very grave look,
Some very 'wise saw' from some very good book, –
  Some such pious divine as St Thomas Aquinas:
  Or, equally charming, The works of Bellarmine;
  Or else he unravels The 'voyages and travels'
Of Hackluytz – (how sadly these Dutch names *do* sully verse!) –
Purchas's, Hawksworth's, or Lemuel Gulliver's, –
Not to name others, 'mongst whom there are few so
Admired as John Bunyan, and Robinson Crusoe. –
  No matter who came, It was always the same,
The Captain was reading aloud to the Dame.
Till, from having gone through half the books on the shelf
They were almost as wise as Sir Thomas himself.
  Well, it happen'd one day, – I really can't say
The particular month: but I think 'twas in May, –
'Twas, I know, in the Spring-time, – when 'Nature looks gay',
As the Poet observes, – and on tree-top and spray
The dear little dickey-birds carol away;
When the grass is so green, and the sun is so bright,
And all things are teeming with life and with light, –
That the whole of the house was thrown into affright,
For no soul could conceive what was gone with the Knight!

  It seems he had taken A light breakfast – bacon,
An egg – with a little broil'd haddock – at most
A round and a half of some hot butter'd toast,
With a slice of cold sirloin from yesterday's roast.
  And then – let me see! – He had two – perhaps three
Cups (with sugar and cream) of strong gunpowder tea,
With a spoonful in each of some choice *eau de vie*,
– Which with nine out of ten would perhaps disagree. –
  – In fact, I and my son Mix 'black' with our 'Hyson',
Neither having the nerves of a bull, or a bison,
And both hating brandy like what some call pison.'

No matter for that – He had call'd for his hat,
With the brim that I've said was so broad and so flat,
And his 'specs' with the tortoiseshell rim, and his cane
With the crutch-handled top, which he used to sustain
His steps in his walks, and to poke in the shrubs
And the grass, when unearthing his worms and his grubs –
Thus arm'd, he set out on a ramble – alack!
He set out, poor dear Soul! – but he never came back.

'First dinner-bell' rang Out its euphonious clang
At five – folks kept early hours then – and the 'Last'
Ding-dong'd, as it ever was wont, at half-past,
        While Betsey and Sally, And Thompson the *Valet*,
And every one else was beginning to bless himself,
Wondering the Knight had not come in to dress himself. –
– Quoth Betsey, 'Dear me! why the fish will be cold!' –
Quoth Sally, 'Good gracious! how "Missis" will scold!'
        Thompson, the *Valet*, Look'd gravely at Sally,
As who should say 'Truth must not always be told!'
Then, expressing a fear least the Knight might take cold,
        Thus exposed to the dews, Lamb's-wool stockings and
            shoes,
        Of each a fresh pair, He put down to air,
And hung a clean shirt to the fire on a chair. –

Still the Master was absent – the Cook came and said, 'he
Much fear'd, as the dinner had been so long ready,
        The roast and the boil'd Would be all of it spoil'd,
And the puddings, her Ladyship thought such a treat,
He was morally sure, would be scarce fit to eat!'
        This closed the debate – "Twould be folly to wait,'
Said the Lady, 'Dish up! – Let the meal be served straight,
And let two or three slices be put on a plate,
And kept hot for Sir Thomas. – He's lost sure as fate!
And, a hundred to one, won't be home till it's late!'
– Captain Dugald MacBride then proceeded to face

The Lady at table, – stood up, and said grace, –
Then set himself down in Sir Thomas's place.

Wearily, wearily, all that night,
    That live-long night did the hours go by;
And the Lady Jane, In grief and in pain,
    She sat herself down to cry!
And Captain MacBride, Who sat by her side,
Though I really can't say that he actually cried,
    At least had a tear in his eye! –
As much as can well be expected perhaps,
From 'very young fellows' for very 'old chaps';
    And if he had said What he'd got in his head,
'Twould have been 'Poor old Buffer! he's certainly dead!'

The morning dawn'd, – and the next, – and the next
And all in the mansion were still perplex'd;
No watch-dog 'bay'd a welcome home,' as
A watch-dog should to the 'Good Sir Thomas';
    No knocker fell His approach to tell,
Not so much as a runaway ring at the bell –
The Hall was silent as Hermit's cell.

Yet the sun shone bright upon tower and tree,
And the meads smiled green as green may be,
And the dear little dickey-birds caroll'd with glee,
And the lambs in the park skipp'd merry and free –
Without, all was joy and harmony!
    'And thus 'twill be, – nor long the day, –
    Ere we, like him, shall pass away!
    Yon Sun, that now *our* bosoms warms,
    Shall shine, – but shine on other forms; –
    Yon Grove, whose choir so sweetly cheers
    Us now, shall sound on other ears, –
    The joyous Lamb, as now, shall play,
    But other eyes its sports survey, –
    The stream we love shall roll as fair,

The flowery sweets, the trim Parterre
Shall scent, as now, the ambient air, –
The Tree, whose bending branches bear
The One loved name – shall yet be there; –
But where the hand that carved it? – Where?'

These were hinted to me as The very ideas
Which pass'd through the mind of the fair Lady Jane,
Her thoughts having taken a sombre-ish train,
As she walk'd on the esplanade, to and again,
    With Captain MacBride, Of course, at her side,
Who could not look quite so forlorn, – though he tried,
– An 'idea', in fact, had got into his head,
That if 'poor dear Sir Thomas' should really be dead,
It might be no bad 'spec.' to be there in his stead,
And, by simply contriving, in due time, to wed
    A Lady who was young and fair,
      A lady slim and tall,
   To set himself down in comfort there
    The Lord of Tapton [1] Hall. –

Thinks he, 'We have sent Half over Kent,
And nobody knows how much money's been spent,
Yet no one's been found to say which way he went! –
    The groom, who's been over to Folkestone and Dover,
Can't get any tidings at all of the rover!
Here's a fortnight and more has gone by, and we've tried
Every plan we could hit on – the whole country-side,
Upon all its dead walls, with placards we've supplied, –
And we've sent round the Crier, and had him well cried –
    "MISSING!! Stolen, or strayed, Lost or mislaid,
A GENTLEMAN; – middle-aged, sober, and staid; –
Stoops slightly; – and when he left home was array'd
In a sad-colour'd suit, somewhat dingy and fray'd; –

1. The familiar abbreviation for Tappington Everard still in use among the tenantry.

Had spectacles on with a tortoiseshell rim,
And a hat rather low-crown'd, and broad in the brim.
    Whoe'ere Shall bear, Or shall send him with care,
(Right side uppermost) home; or shall give notice where
The said middle-aged GENTLEMAN is; or shall state
Any fact, that may tend to throw light on his fate,
To the man at the turnpike, called TAPPINGTON GATE,
Shall receive a REWARD of FIVE POUNDS for his trouble,
(☞ N.B. – If defunct the REWARD will be double!! ☜)"

'Had he been above ground He *must* have been found.
No; doubtless he's shot, – or he's hanged, – or he's drown'd!
    Then his Widow – ay! ay! – But what will folks say! –
To address her at once – at so early a day!
Well – what then? – who cares! – let 'em say what they may –
A fig for their nonsense and chatter! – suffice it, her
Charms will excuse one for casting sheep's eyes at her!'

When a man has decided As Captain MacBride did,
And once fully made up his mind on the matter, he
Can't be too prompt in unmasking his battery.
He began on the instant, and vow'd that 'her eyes
Far exceeded in brilliance the stars in the skies, –
That her lips were like roses – her cheeks were like lilies –
Her breath had the odour of daffy-down-dillies!' –
With a thousand more compliments equally true,
And expressed in similitudes equally new!
    – Then his left arm he placed Round her jimp, taper waste –
– Ere she fixed to repulse, or return, his embrace,
Up came running a man, at a deuce of a pace,
With that very peculiar expression of face
Which always betokens dismay or disaster,
Crying out – 'twas the Gardener, – 'Oh, Ma'am! we've found
    Master!'
– 'Where! where?' screamed the lady: and Echo scream'd
    'Where?'

The man couldn't say 'There!' He had no breath to spare,
But, gasping for air, he could only respond
By pointing – he pointed, alas! – TO THE POND.
– 'Twas e'en so – poor dear Knight! – with his 'specs' and his
    hat
He'd gone poking his nose into this and to that;
    When, close to the side Of the bank he espied
An 'uncommon fine' Tadpole, remarkably fat!
    He stoop'd; and he thought her
    His own; he had caught her!
Got hold of her tail, – and to land almost brought her,
When – he plump'd head and heels into fifteen feet water!

    The Lady Jane was tall and slim,
      The Lady Jane was fair,
    Alas for Sir Thomas! – she grieved for him,.
      As she saw two serving-men, sturdy of limb,
      His body between them bear,
She sobb'd, and she sigh'd; she lamented, and cried,
    For of sorrow brimful was her cup;
She swoon'd, and I think she'd have fall'n down and died,
    If Captain MacBride Had not been by her side,
With the Gardener; they both their assistance supplied,
    And managed to hold her up. –
    But when she 'comes to', Oh! 'tis shocking to view
    The sight which the corpse reveals!
    Sir Thomas's body, It looked so odd – he
    Was half eaten up by the eels!
His waistcoat and hose, and the rest of his clothes
    Were all gnaw'd through and through;
    And out of each shoe An eel they drew;
And from each of his pockets they pull'd out two
And the Gardener himself had secreted a few,
    As well we may suppose;
For, when he came running to give the alarm,
He had six in the basket that hung on his arm.

Good Father John Was summon'd anon;
Holy water was sprinkled, And little bells tinkled,
And tapers were lighted, And incense ignited,
And masses were sung, and masses were said,
All day, for the quiet repose of the dead,
And all night no one thought about going to bed.

But Lady Jane was tall and slim,
And Lady Jane was fair, –
And, ere morning came, that winsome dame
Had made up her mind – or, what's much the same,
Had *thought about* – once more 'changing her name',
And she said, with a pensive air,
To Thompson, the valet, while taking away,
When supper was over, the cloth and the tray, –
'Eels a many I've ate; but any
So good ne'er tasted before! –
They're a fish, too, of which I'm remarkably fond, –
Go – pop Sir Thomas again in the Pond –
Poor dear! – HE'LL CATCH US SOME MORE!!'

MORAL

All middle-aged Gentlemen let me advise,
If you're married, and have not got very good eyes,
Don't go poking about after blue-bottle flies! –
If you've spectacles, don't have a tortoiseshell rim,
And don't go near the water, – unless you can swim!

Married Ladies, especially such as are fair,
Tall, and slim, I would next recommend to beware
How, on losing one spouse, they give way to despair;
But let them reflect 'There are fish, and no doubt on't –
As good in the river as ever came out on't!'

Should they light on a spouse who is given to roaming
In solitude – *raison de plus*, in the 'gloaming', –
Let them have a fix'd time for said spouse to come home in!
And if, when 'last dinner-bell's' rung, he is late,
To insure better manners in future – Don't wait! –
If of husband or children they chance to be fond,
Have a stout iron-wire fence put all round the pond!

One more piece of advice, and I close my appeals –
That is – if you chance to be partial to eels,
Then – *Crede experto* – trust one who has tried –
Have them spitch-cock'd – or stew'd – they're too oily when
    fried!

R. H. BARHAM

Hon. Mr Sucklethumbkin's Story

THE EXECUTION

A Sporting Anecdote

My Lord Tomnoddy got up one day;
   It was half after two, He had nothing to do,
So his Lordship rang for his cabriolet.

   Tiger Tim Was clean of limb,
His boots were polish'd, his jacket was trim;
With a very smart tie in his smart cravat,
And a smart cockade on the top of his hat;
Tallest of boys, or shortest of men,
He stood in his stockings just four foot ten;
And he ask'd, as he held the door on the swing,
'Pray, did your Lordship please to ring?'

My Lord Tomnoddy he raised his head,
And thus to Tiger Tim he said,

'Malibran's dead, Duvernay's fled,
Taglioni has not yet arrived in her stead;
Tiger Tim, come tell me true,
What may a Nobleman find to do? –

Tim look'd up, and Tim look'd down,
He paused, and he put on a thoughtful frown,
And he held up his hat, and he peep'd in the crown;
He bit his lip, and he scratch'd his head,
He let go the handle, and thus he said,
As the door, released, behind him bang'd:
'An't please you, my Lord, there's a man to be hang'd.'

My Lord Tomnoddy jump'd up at the news,
    'Run to M'Fuze, And Lieutenant Tregooze,
And run to Sir Carnaby Jenks, of the Blues.
    Rope-dancers a score I've seen before –
Madame Sacchi, Antonio, and Master Black-more;
    But to see a man swing At the end of a string,
With his neck in a noose, will be quite a new thing!'

My Lord Tomnoddy stept into his cab –
Dark rifle green, with a lining of drab;
    Through street and through square,
    His high-trotting mare,
Like one of Ducrow's, goes pawing the air.
Adown Piccadilly and Waterloo Place
Went the high-trotting mare at a very quick pace;
    She produced some alarm. But did no great harm,
Save frightening a nurse with a child on her arm,
    Spattering with clay Two urchins at play,
Knocking down – very much to the sweeper's dismay –
An old woman who wouldn't get out of the way,
    And upsetting a stall Near Exeter Hall,
Which made all the pious Church-Mission folks squall.
    But eastward afar Through Temple Bar,

My Lord Tomnoddy directs his car;
　　Never heeding their squalls,
　　Or their calls, or their bawls,
He passes by Waithman's Emporium for shawls,
And, merely just catching a glimpse of St Paul's,
　　Turns down the Old Bailey,
　　Where in front of the gaol, he
Pulls up at the door of the gin-shop, and gaily
Cries, 'What must I fork out to-night, my trump,
For the whole first-floor of the Magpie and Stump?'

*

The clock strikes Twelve – it is dark midnight –
Yet the Magpie and Stump is one blaze of light,
　　The parties are met; The tables are set;
There is 'punch', 'cold without', 'hot with', 'heavy wet,'
　　Ale-glasses and jugs, And rummers and mugs,
And sand on the floor, without carpets or rugs,
　　Cold fowl and cigars, Pickled onions in jars,
Welsh rabbits and kidneys – rare work for the jaws: –
And very large lobsters, with very large claws;
　　And there is M'Fuze, And Lieutenant Tregooze;
And there is Sir Carnaby Jenks, of the Blues,
All come to see a man 'die in his shoes!'

　　The clock strikes One! Supper is done,
And Sir Carnaby Jenks is full of his fun,
Singing 'Jolly companions every one!'
　　My Lord Tomnoddy Is drinking gin-toddy,
And laughing at ev'ry thing, and ev'ry body. –

The clock strikes Two! and the clock strikes Three!
– 'Who so merry, so merry as we?'
　　Save Captain M'Fuze, Who is taking a snooze,
While Sir Carnaby Jenks is busy at work,
Blacking his nose with a piece of burnt cork.

The clock strikes Four! – Round the debtors' door
Are gather'd a couple of thousand or more;
    As many await At the press-yard gate,
Till slowly its folding doors open, and straight
The mob divides, and between their ranks
A wagon comes loaded with posts and with planks.

The clock strikes Five! The Sheriffs arrive,
And the crowd is so great that the street seems alive;
    But Sir Carnaby Jenks Blinks, and winks,
A candle burns down in the socket, and stinks.
    Lieutenant Tregooze Is dreaming of Jews,
And acceptances all the bill-brokers refuse;
    My Lord Tomnoddy Has drunk all his toddy,
And just as the dawn is beginning to peep,
The whole of the party are fast asleep.

Sweetly, oh! sweetly, the morning breaks,
    With roseate streaks,
Like the first faint blush on a maiden's cheeks;
Seem'd as that mild and clear blue sky
Smiled upon all things far and high,
On all – save the wretch condemn'd to die!
Alack! that ever so fair a Sun,
As that which its course has now begun,
Should rise on such a scene of misery! –
Should gild with rays so light and free
That dismal, dark-frowning Gallows-tree!

And hark! – a sound comes, big with fate;
The clock from St Sepulchre's tower strikes – Eight! –
List to that low funereal bell:
It is tolling, alas! a living man's knell! –
And see! – from forth that opening door
They come – He steps that threshold o'er
Who never shall tread upon threshold more!

– God! 'tis a fearsome thing to see
That pale wan man's mute agony, –
The glare of that wild, despairing eye,
Now bent on the crowd, now turn'd to the sky
As though 'twere scanning, in doubt and in fear,
The path of the Spirit's unknown career;
Those pinion'd arms, those hands that ne'er
Shall be lifted again, – not even in prayer;
That heaving chest! Enough – 'tis done!
The bolt has fallen! – the spirit is gone –
For weal or for woe is known but to One! –
– Oh! 'twas a fearsome sight! Ah me!
A deed to shudder at, – not to see.

Again that clock! 'tis time, 'tis time!
The hour is past: with its earliest chime
The cord is severed, the lifeless clay
By 'dungeon villains' is borne away:
Nine! 'twas the last concluding stroke!
And then – my Lord Tomnoddy awoke!
And Tregooze and Sir Carnaby Jenks arose,
And Captain M'Fuze, with the black on his nose:
And they stared at each other, as much as to say
    'Hollo! Hollo! Here's a rum Go!
Why, Captain! – my Lord! – Here's the devil to pay!
The fellow's been cut down and taken away!
    What's to be done? We've miss'd all the fun! –
Why, they'll laugh at and quiz us all over the town
We are all of us done so uncommonly brown!'

What was to be done? – 'twas perfectly plain
That they could not well hang the man over again:
What was to be done? – The man was dead!
Nought could be done – nought could be said;
So – my Lord Tomnoddy went home to bed!

                                R. H. BARHAM

The Lamentable Ballad of the Foundling of Shoreditch

Come all ye Christian people, and listen to my tail
   It is all about a doctor was travelling by the rail,
     By the Heastern Counties Railway (vich the shares I don't
       desire,)
From Ixworth town in Suffolk, vich his name did not transpire.

A travelling from Bury this Doctor was employed
With a gentleman, a friend of his, vich his name was Captain
     Lloyd,
And on reaching Marks Tey Station, that is next beyond Colchester,
     a lady entered in to them most elegantly dressed.

She entered into the Carriage all with a tottering step,
And a pooty little Bayby upon her bussum slep;
The gentlemen received her with kindness and siwillaty,
Pitying this lady for her illness and debillaty.

She had a fust-class ticket, this lovely lady said;
Because it was so lonesome she took a secknd instead.
Better to travel by secknd class, than sit alone in the fust,
And the pooty little Baby upon her breast she nust.

A seein of her cryin, and shiverin and pail,
To her spoke this surging, the Ero of my tail;
Saysee 'You look unwell, ma'am: I'll elp you if I can,
And you may tell your case to me, for I'm a meddicle man.'

'Thank you, sir,' the lady said, 'I only look so pale,
Because I ain't accustom'd to travelling on the Rale;
I shall be better presnly, when I've ad some rest:'
And that pooty little Baby she squeeged it to her breast.

So in conversation the journey they beguiled,
Capting Loyd and the meddicle man, and the lady and the child,
Till the warious stations along the line was passed,
For even the Heastern Counties' trains must come in at last.

When at Shoreditch tumminus at length stopped the train,
This kind meddicle gentleman proposed his aid again.
'Thank you, sir,' the lady said, 'for your kyindness dear;
My carridge and my osses is probibbly come here.

'Will you old this baby, please, vilst I step and see?'
The Doctor was a family man: 'That I will,' says he.
Then the little child she kist, kist it very gently,
Vich was sucking his little fist, sleeping innocently.

With a sigh from her art, as though she would have bust it,
Then she gave the Doctor the child – wery kind he nust it:
Hup then the lady jumped hoff the bench she sat from,
Tumbled down the carridge steps and ran along the platform.

Vile hall the other passengers vent upon their vays,
The Capting and the Doctor sat there in a maze;
Some vent in a Homminibus, some vent in a Cabby,
The Capting and the Doctor vaited vith the babby.

There they sat looking queer, for an hour or more,
But their feller passinger neather on 'em sore:
Never, never back again did that lady come
To that pooty sleeping Hinfnt a suckin' of his Thum!

What could this pore Doctor do, bein' treated thus,
When the darling Baby woke, cryin' for its nuss?
Off he drove to a female friend, vich she was both kind and mild,
And igsplained to her the circumstance of this year little child.

That kind lady took the child instantly in her lap,
And made it very comfortable by giving it some pap;
And when she took its close off, what d'you think she found?
A couple of ten pun notes sewn up in its little gownd!

Also in its little close, was a note which did conwey,
That this little baby's parents lived in a handsome way
And for its Headucation they reglarly would pay,
And sirtingly like gentlefolks would claim the child one day,
If the Christian people who'd charge of it would say,
Per adwertisement in *The Times*, where the baby lay.

Pity of this bayby many people took,
It had such pooty ways and such a pooty look;
And there came a lady forrard (I wish that I could see
Any kind lady as would do as much for me;

And I wish with all my art, some night in my night gownd,
I could find a note stitched for ten or twenty pound) –
There came a lady forrard, that most honorable did say,
She'd adopt this little baby, which her parents cast away.

While the Doctor pondered on this hoffer fair,
Comes a letter from Devonshire, from a party there,
Hordering the Doctor, at its Mar's desire,
To send the little Infant back to Devonshire.

Lost in apoplexity, this pore meddicle man,
Like a sensable gentleman, to the Justice ran,
Which his name was Mr Hammill, a honorable beak,
That takes his seat in Worship Street four times a week.

'O Justice!' says the Doctor, 'instrugt me what to do.
I've come up from the country, to throw myself on you;
My patients have no doctor to tend them in their ills
(There they are in Suffolk without their draffts and pills!).

'I've come up from the country, to know how I'll dispose
Of this pore little baby, and the twenty pun note, and the close,
And I want to go back to Suffolk, dear Justice, if you please,
And my patients wants their Doctor, and their Doctor wants his
   feez.'

Up spoke Mr Hammill, sittin' at his desk,
'This year application does me much perplesk;
What I do adwise you, is to leave this babby
In the Parish where it was left by its mother shabby.'

The Doctor from his Worship sadly did depart —
He might have left the baby, but he hadn't got the heart
To go for to leave that Hinnocent, has the laws allows,
To the tender mussies of the Union House.

Mother, who left this little one on a stranger's knee,
Think how cruel you have been, and how good was he!
Think, if you've been guilty, innocent was she;
And do not take unkindly this little word of me:
Heaven be merciful to us all, sinners as we be!

W. M. THACKERAY

The Ballad of the Oysterman

It was a tall young oysterman lived by the river-side,
His shop was just upon the bank, his boat was on the tide;
The daughter of a fisherman, that was so straight and slim,
Lived over on the other bank, right opposite to him.

It was the pensive oysterman that saw a lovely maid,
Upon a moonlight evening, a-sitting in the shade!
He saw her wave her handkerchief, as much as if to say,
'I'm wide awake, young oysterman, and all the folks away.'

Then up arose the oysterman, and to himself said he,
'I guess I'll leave the skiff at home, for fear that folks should see;
I read it in the story-book, that, for to kiss his dear,
Leander swam the Hellespont – and I will swim this here.'

And he has leaped into the waves, and crossed the shining stream,
And he has clambered up the bank, all in the moonlight gleam;
Oh, there were kisses sweet as dew, and words as soft as rain, –
But they have heard her father's step, and in he leaps again!

Out spoke the ancient fisherman: 'Oh, what was that, my
       daughter?'
''Twas nothing but a pebble, sir, I threw into the water.'
'And what is that, pray tell me, love, that paddles off so fast?'
'It's nothing but a porpoise, sir, that's been a-swimming past.'

Out spoke the ancient fisherman: 'Now bring me my harpoon!
I'll get into my fishing-boat, and fix the fellow soon.'
Down fell that pretty innocent, as falls a snow-white lamb!
Her hair drooped round her pallid cheeks, like seaweed on a clam.

Alas for those two loving ones! she waked not from her swouned,
And he was taken with the cramp, and in the waves was drowned!
But Fate has metamorphosed them, in pity of their woe,
And now they keep an oyster-shop for mermaids down below.

                                    OLIVER WENDELL HOLMES

                  Hertfordshire Harmony

            There was an old fellow of Tring
            Who, when somebody asked him to sing,
                  Replied, 'Ain't it odd?
                  I can never tell *God*
            Save the Weasel from *Pop goes the King*.'

                                    ANON.

Saying Not Meaning

Two gentlemen their appetite had fed,
When, opening his toothpick-case, one said –
'It was not until lately that I knew
That anchovies on terra firma grew.'
' Grow!' cried the other: 'yes, they grow indeed,
Like other fish, but not upon the land;
You might as well say grapes grow on a reed
　　Or in the Strand.'

'Why, sir,' returned the irritated other,
　　　'My brother,
　　When at Calcutta
Beheld them, bonâ fide growing!
　　He wouldn't utter
A lie for love or money, sir; and so in
　　This matter you are thoroughly mistaken.'
'Nonsense, sir, nonsense! I can give no credit
To the assertion; none e'er saw or read it;
　　Your brother, like his evidence, should be shaken.'

'Be shaken, sir! Let me observe, you are perverse.
　　　In short' –
'Sir,' said the other, sucking his cigar,
　　And then his port,
'If you will say impossibles are true,
　　You may affirm just anything you please –
That swans are quadrupeds, and lions blue,
　　And elephants inhabit Stilton cheese;
Only you must not force me to believe
What's propagated merely to deceive.'

'Then you force me to say, sir, you're a fool.'
　　Returned the bragger.

Language like this no man can suffer cool:
   It made the listener stagger.
So, thunder-stricken, he at once replied,
   'The traveller lied
Who had the impudence to tell it you.'

'Zounds! then, d'ye mean to swear before my face
That anchovies don't grow, like cloves and mace?'
   'I do!'
Disputants often, after hot debates,
   Leave the contention as they found it – bone,
And take to duelling, or thumping têtes,
   Thinking by strength of artery to atone
For strength of argument; and he who winces
From force of words, with force of arms convinces!

With pistols, powder, bullets, surgeons, lint,
Seconds, and smelling-bottles, and foreboding,
Our friends advanced; and now portentous loading
(Their hearts already loaded) served to show
It might be better they shook hands – but no;
When each opines himself, though frightened right,
Each is, in courtesy, obliged to fight.

And they did fight: from six full-measured paces
   The unbeliever pulled his trigger first,
And fearing, from the braggart's ugly faces,
   The whizzing lead had whizzed its very worst,
Ran up, and with a duelistic fear,
   His ire evanishing like morning vapours,
Found him possessed of one remaining ear:
Who, in a manner sudden and uncouth,
Had given, not lent, the other ear to truth.
For while the surgeon was applying lint,
He, wriggling, cried – 'The deuce is in't –
   'Sir! I meant capers!'

WILLIAM BASIL WAKE

The Hunting of the Snark

FIT THE FIRST
The Landing

'Just the place for a Snark!' the Bellman cried,
    As he landed his crew with care;
Supporting each man on the top of the tide
    By a finger entwined in his hair.

'Just the place for a Snark! I have said it twice:
    That alone should encourage the crew.
Just the place for a Snark! I have said it thrice:
    What I tell you three times is true.'

The crew was complete: it included a Boots –
    A maker of Bonnets and Hoods –
A Barrister, brought to arrange their disputes –
    And a Broker, to value their goods.

A Billiard-marker, whose skill was immense,
    Might perhaps have won more than his share –
But a Banker, engaged at enormous expense,
    Had the whole of their cash in his care.

There was also a Beaver, that paced on the deck,
    Or would sit making lace in the bow:
And had often (the Bellman said) saved them from wreck,
    Though none of the sailors knew how.

There was one who was famed for the number of things
    He forgot when he entered the ship:
His umbrella, his watch, all his jewels and rings,
    And the clothes he had bought for the trip.

He had forty-two boxes, all carefully packed,
  With his name painted clearly on each:
But, since he omitted to mention the fact,
  They were all left behind on the beach.

The loss of his clothes hardly mattered, because
  He had seven coats on when he came,
With three pair of boots – but the worst of it was,
  He had wholly forgotten his name.

He would answer to 'Hi!' or to any loud cry,
  Such as 'Fry me!' or 'Fritter my wig!'
To 'What-you-may-call-um!' or 'What-was-his-name!'
  But especially 'Thing-um-a-jig!'

While, for those who preferred a more forcible word,
  He had different names from these:
His intimate friends called him 'Candle-ends,'
  And his enemies 'Toasted-cheese.'

'His form is ungainly – his intellect small –'
  (So the Bellman would often remark)
'But his courage is perfect! And that, after all,
  Is the thing that one needs with a Snark.'

He would joke with hyaenas, returning their stare
  With an impudent wag of the head:
And he once went a walk, paw-in-paw, with a bear,
  'Just to keep up its spirits,' he said.

He came as a Baker: but owned when too late –
  And it drove the poor Bellman half-mad –
He could only bake Bridecake – for which, I may state,
  No materials were to be had.

The last of the crew needs especial remark,
  Though he looked an incredible dunce:

He had just one idea – but, that one being 'Snark',
  The good Bellman engaged him at once.

He came as a Butcher: but gravely declared,
  When the ship had been sailing a week,
He could only kill Beavers. The Bellman looked scared,
  And was almost too frightened to speak:

But at length he explained, in a tremulous tone,
  There was only one Beaver on board;
And that was a tame one he had of his own,
  Whose death would be deeply deplored.

The Beaver, who happened to hear the remark,
  Protested, with tears in its eyes,
That not even the rapture of hunting the Snark
  Could atone for that dismal surprise!

It strongly advised that the Butcher should be
  Conveyed in a separate ship:
But the Bellman declared that would never agree
  With the plans he had made for the trip:

Navigation was always a difficult art,
  Though with only one ship and one bell:
And he feared he must really decline, for his part,
  Undertaking another as well.

The Beaver's best course was, no doubt, to procure
  A second-hand dagger-proof coat –
So the Baker advised it – and next, to insure
  Its life in some Office of note:

This the Banker suggested, and offered for hire
  (On moderate terms), or for sale,
Two excellent Policies, one Against Fire,
  And one Against Damage from Hail.

Yet still, ever after that sorrowful day,
   Whenever the Butcher was by,
The Beaver kept looking the opposite way,
   And appeared unaccountably shy.

FIT THE SECOND

The Bellman's Speech

The Bellman himself they all praised to the skies —
   Such a carriage, such ease and such grace!
Such solemnity, too! One could see he was wise,
   The moment one looked in his face!

He had bought a large map representing the sea,
   Without the least vestige of land:
And the crew were much pleased when they found it to be
   A map they could all understand.

'What's the good of Mercator's North Poles and Equators,
   Tropics, Zones and Meridian Lines?'
So the Bellman would cry: and the crew would reply
   'They are merely conventional signs!

'Other maps are such shapes, with their islands and capes!
   But we've got our brave Captain to thank'
(So the crew would protest) 'that he's bought us the best —
   A perfect and absolute blank!'

This was charming, no doubt: but they shortly found out
   That the Captain they trusted so well
Had only one notion for crossing the ocean,
   And that was to tingle his bell.

He was thoughtful and grave — but the orders he gave
   Were enough to bewilder a crew.

When he cried, 'Steer to starboard, but keep her head lar-
        board!'
    What on earth was the helmsman to do?

Then the bowsprit got mixed with the rudder sometimes:
    A thing, as the Bellman remarked,
That frequently happens in tropical climes,
    When a vessel is, so to speak, 'snarked'.

But the principal failing occurred in the sailing,
    And the Bellman, perplexed and distressed,
Said he had hoped, at least, when the wind blew due East
    That the ship would not travel due West!

But the danger was past – they had landed at last,
    With their boxes, portmanteaux, and bags:
Yet at first sight the crew were not pleased with the view,
    Which consisted of chasms and crags.

The Bellman perceived that their spirits were low,
    And repeated in musical tone
Some jokes he had kept for a season of woe –
    But the crew would do nothing but groan.

He served out some grog with a liberal hand,
    And bade them sit down on the beach:
And they could not but own that their Captain looked grand,
    As he stood and delivered his speech.

'Friends, Romans, and countrymen, lend me your ears!'
    (They were all of them fond of quotations:
So they drank to his health, and they gave him three cheers,
    While he served out additional rations.)

'We have sailed many months, we have sailed many weeks
    (Four weeks to the month you may mark),

But never as yet ('tis your Captain who speaks)
    Have we caught the least glimpse of a Snark!

'We have sailed many weeks, we have sailed many days
    (Seven days to the week I allow),
But a Snark, on the which we might lovingly gaze,
    We have never beheld till now!

'Come, listen, my men, while I tell you again
    The five unmistakable marks
By which you may know, wheresoever you go,
    The warranted genuine Snarks.

'Let us take them in order. The first is the taste,
    Which is meagre and hollow, but crisp:
Like a coat that is rather too tight in the waist,
    With a flavour of Will-o'-the-wisp.

'Its habit of getting up late you'll agree
    That it carries too far, when I say
That it frequently breakfasts at five-o'clock tea,
    And dines on the following day.

'The third is its slowness in taking a jest,
    Should you happen to venture on one,
It will sigh like a thing that is deeply distressed:
    And it always looks grave at a pun.

'The fourth is its fondness for bathing-machines,
    Which it constantly carries about,
And believes that they add to the beauty of scenes —
    A sentiment open to doubt.

'The fifth is ambition. It next will be right
    To describe each particular batch:
Distinguishing those that have feathers, and bite,
    From those that have whiskers, and scratch.

'For, although common Snarks do no manner of harm,
    Yet, I feel it my duty to say,
Some are Boojums – ' The Bellman broke off in alarm,
    For the Baker had fainted away.

FIT THE THIRD

The Baker's Tale

They roused him with muffins – they roused him with ice –
    They roused him with mustard and cress –
They roused him with jam and judicious advice –
    They set him conundrums to guess.

When at length he sat up and was able to speak,
    His sad story he offered to tell;
And the Bellman cried, 'Silence! not even a shriek!'
    And excitedly tingled his bell.

There was silence supreme! Not a shriek, not a scream,
    Scarcely even a howl or a groan,
As the man they called 'Ho!' told his story of woe
    In an antediluvian tone.

'My father and mother were honest, though poor – '
    'Skip all that!' cried the Bellman in haste.
'If it once becomes dark, there's no chance of a Snark –
    We have hardly a minute to waste!'

'I skip forty years,' said the Baker, in tears,
    'And proceed without further remark
To the day when you took me aboard of your ship
    To help you in hunting the Snark.

'A dear uncle of mine (after whom I was named)
    Remarked, when I bade him farewell – '

'Oh, skip your dear uncle!' the Bellman exclaimed,
  As he angrily tingled his bell.

'He remarked to me then,' said that mildest of men,
  ' "If your Snark be a Snark, that is right:
Fetch it home by all means – you may serve it with greens,
  And it's handy for striking a light.

' "You may seek it with thimbles – and seek it with care;
  You may hunt it with forks and hope;
You may threaten its life with a railway-share;
  You may charm it with smiles and soap – " '

('That's exactly the method,' the Bellman bold
  In a hasty parenthesis cried,
'That's exactly the way I have always been told
  That the capture of Snarks should be tried!')

' "But oh, beamish nephew, beware of the day,
  If your Snark be a Boojum! For then
You will softly and suddenly vanish away,
  And never be met with again!"

'It is this, it is this that oppresses my soul,
  When I think of my uncle's last words:
And my heart is like nothing so much as a bowl
  Brimming over with quivering curds!

'It is this, it is this – ' 'We have had that before!'
  The Bellman indignantly said.
And the Baker replied, 'Let me say it once more.
  It is this, it is this that I dread!

'I engage with the Snark – every night after dark –
  In a dreamy delirious fight:
I serve it with greens in those shadowy scenes,
  And I use it for striking a light;

'But if ever I meet with a Boojum, that day,
    In a moment (of this I am sure),
I shall softly and suddenly vanish away —
    And the notion I cannot endure!'

FIT THE FOURTH

The Hunting

The Bellman looked uffish, and wrinkled his brow.
    'If only you'd spoken before!
It's excessively awkward to mention it now,
    With the Snark, so to speak, at the door!

'We should all of us grieve, as you well may believe,
    If you never were met with again —
But surely, my man, when the voyage began,
    You might have suggested it then?

'It's excessively awkward to mention it now —
    As I think I've already remarked.'
And the man they called 'Hi!' replied, with a sigh,
    'I informed you the day we embarked.

'You may charge me with murder — or want of sense —
    (We are all of us weak at times):
But the slightest approach to a false pretence
    Was never among my crimes!

'I said it in Hebrew — I said it in Dutch —
    I said it in German and Greek;
But I wholly forgot (and it vexes me much)
    That English is what you speak!'

''Tis a pitiful tale,' said the Bellman, whose face
    Had grown longer at every word;

'But, now that you've stated the whole of your case,
　　More debate would be simply absurd.

'The rest of my speech' (he explained to his men)
　　'You shall hear when I've leisure to speak it.
But the Snark is at hand, let me tell you again!
　　'Tis your glorious duty to seek it!

'To seek it with thimbles, to seek it with care;
　　To pursue it with forks and hope;
To threaten its life with a railway-share;
　　To charm it with smiles and soap!

'For the Snark's a peculiar creature, that won't
　　Be caught in a commonplace way.
Do all that you know, and try all that you don't:
　　Not a chance must be wasted to-day!

'For England expects – I forbear to proceed:
　　'Tis a maxim tremendous, but trite:
And you'd best be unpacking the things that you need
　　To rig yourselves out for the fight.'

Then the Banker endorsed a blank cheque (which he crossed),
　　And changed his loose silver for notes.
The Baker with care combed his whiskers and hair,
　　And shook the dust out of his coats.

The Boots and the Broker were sharpening a spade –
　　Each working the grindstone in turn;
But the Beaver went on making lace, and displayed
　　No interest in the concern:

Though the Barrister tried to appeal to its pride,
　　And vainly proceeded to cite
A number of cases, in which making laces
　　Had been proved an infringement of right.

The maker of Bonnets ferociously planned
 A novel arrangement of bows:
While the Billiard-marker with quivering hand
 Was chalking the tip of his nose.

But the Butcher turned nervous, and dressed himself fine,
 With yellow kid gloves and a ruff —
Said he felt it exactly like going to dine,
 Which the Bellman declared was all 'stuff'.

'Introduce me, now there's a good fellow,' he said,
 'If we happen to meet it together!'
And the Bellman, sagaciously nodding his head,
 Said, 'That must depend on the weather.'

The Beaver went simply galumphing about,
 At seeing the Butcher so shy:
And even the Baker, though stupid and stout,
 Made an effort to wink with one eye.

'Be a man!' said the Bellman in wrath, as he heard
 The Butcher beginning to sob.
'Should we meet with a Jubjub, that desperate bird,
 We shall need all our strength for the job!'

FIT THE FIFTH

The Beaver's Lesson

They sought it with thimbles, they sought it with care;
 They pursued it with forks and hope;
They threatened its life with a railway-share;
 They charmed it with smiles and soap.

Then the Butcher contrived an ingenious plan
 For making a separate sally;

And had fixed on a spot unfrequented by man,
    A dismal and desolate valley.

But the very same plan to the Beaver occurred:
    It had chosen the very same place;
Yet neither betrayed, by a sign or a word,
    The disgust that appeared in his face.

Each thought he was thinking of nothing but 'Snark'
    And the glorious work of the day;
And each tried to pretend that he did not remark
    That the other was going that way.

But the valley grew narrow and narrower still,
    And the evening got darker and colder,
Till (merely from nervousness, not from goodwill)
    They marched along shoulder to shoulder.

Then a scream, shrill and high, rent the shuddering sky,
    And they knew that some danger was near:
The Beaver turned pale to the tip of its tail,
    And even the Butcher felt queer.

He thought of his childhood, left far far behind —
    That blissful and innocent state —
The sound so exactly recalled to his mind
    A pencil that squeaks on a slate!

"'Tis the voice of the Jubjub!' he suddenly cried.
    (This man, that they used to call 'Dunce'.)
'As the Bellman would tell you,' he added with pride,
    'I have uttered that sentiment once.

"'Tis the note of the Jubjub! Keep count, I entreat;
    You will find I have told it you twice.
'Tis the song of the Jubjub! The proof is complete,
    If only I've stated it thrice.'

The Beaver had counted with scrupulous care,
  Attending to every word:
But it fairly lost heart, and outgrabe in despair,
  When the third repetition occurred.

It felt that, in spite of all possible pains,
  It had somehow contrived to lose count,
And the only thing now was to rack its poor brains
  By reckoning up the amount.

'Two added to one — if that could but be done,'
  It said, 'with one's fingers and thumbs!'
Recollecting with tears how, in earlier years,
  It had taken no pains with its sums.

'The thing can be done,' said the Butcher, 'I think.
  The thing must be done, I am sure.
The thing shall be done! Bring me paper and ink,
  The best there is time to procure.'

The Beaver brought paper, portfolio, pens,
  And ink in unfailing supplies:
While strange creepy creatures came out of their dens,
  And watched them with wondering eyes.

So engrossed was the Butcher, he heeded them not,
  As he wrote with a pen in each hand,
And explained all the while in a popular style
  Which the Beaver could well understand.

'Taking Three as the subject to reason about —
  A convenient number to state —
We add Seven, and Ten, and then multiply out
  By One Thousand diminished by Eight.

'The result we proceed to divide, as you see,
  By Nine Hundred and Ninety and Two:

Then subtract Seventeen, and the answer must be
    Exactly and perfectly true.

'The method employed I would gladly explain,
    While I have it so clear in my head,
If I had but the time and you had but the brain –
    But much yet remains to be said.

'In one moment I've seen what has hitherto been
    Enveloped in absolute mystery,
And without extra charge I will give you at large
    A Lesson in Natural History.'

In his genial way he proceeded to say
    (Forgetting all laws of propriety,
And that giving instruction, without introduction,
    Would have caused quite a thrill in Society).

'As to temper the Jubjub's a desperate bird,
    Since it lives in perpetual passion:
Its taste in costume is entirely absurd –
    It is ages ahead of the fashion:

'But it knows any friend it has met once before:
    It never will look at a bribe:
And in charity-meetings it stands at the door,
    And collects – though it does not subscribe.

'Its flavour when cooked is more exquisite far
    Than mutton, or oysters, or eggs:
(Some think it keeps best in an ivory jar,
    And some, in mahogany kegs):

You boil it in sawdust: you salt it in glue:
    You condense it with locusts and tape:
Still keeping one principal object in view –
    To preserve its symmetrical shape.'

The Butcher would gladly have talked till next day,
    But he felt that the lesson must end,
And he wept with delight in attempting to say
    He considered the Beaver his friend.

While the Beaver confessed, with affectionate looks
    More eloquent even than tears,
It had learnt in ten minutes far more than all books
    Would have taught it in seventy years.

They returned hand-in-hand, and the Bellman, unmanned
    (For a moment) with noble emotion,
Said, 'This amply repays all the wearisome days
    We have spent on the billowy ocean!'

Such friends, as the Beaver and Butcher became,
    Have seldom if ever been known;
In winter or summer, 'twas always the same –
    You could never meet either alone.

And when quarrels arose – as one frequently finds
    Quarrels will, spite of every endeavour –
The song of the Jubjub recurred to their minds,
    And cemented their friendship for ever!

FIT THE SIXTH

The Barrister's Dream

They sought it with thimbles, they sought it with care:
    They pursued it with forks and hope;
They threatened its life with a railway-share:
    They charmed it with smiles and soap.

But the Barrister, weary of proving in vain
    That the Beaver's lace-making was wrong,

Fell asleep, and in dreams saw the creature quite plain
    That his fancy had dwelt on so long.

He dreamed that he stood in a shadowy Court,
    Where the Snark, with a glass in its eye,
Dressed in gown, bands, and wig, was defending a pig
    On the charge of deserting its sty.

The Witnesses proved, without error or flaw,
    That the sty was deserted when found:
And the Judge kept explaining the state of the law
    In a soft under-current of sound.

The indictment had never been clearly expressed,
    And it seemed that the Snark had begun,
And had spoken three hours, before anyone guessed
    What the pig was supposed to have done.

The Jury had each formed a different view
    (Long before the indictment was read),
And they all spoke at once, so that none of them knew
    One word that the others had said.

'You must know – ' said the Judge: but the Snark exclaimed,
    'Fudge!
    That statute is obsolete quite!
Let me tell you, my friends, the whole question depends
    On an ancient manorial right.

'In the matter of Treason the pig would appear
    To have aided, but scarcely abetted:
While the charge of Insolvency fails, it is clear,
    If you grant the plea "never indebted".

'The fact of Desertion I will not dispute:
    But its guilt, as I trust, is removed

(So far as relates to the costs of this suit)
    By the Alibi which has been proved.

'My poor client's fate now depends on your votes.'
    Here the speaker sat down in his place,
And directed the Judge to refer to his notes
    And briefly to sum up the case.

But the Judge said he never had summed up before;
    So the Snark undertook it instead,
And summed it so well that it came to far more
    Than the Witnesses ever had said!

When the verdict was called for, the Jury declined,
    As the word was so puzzling to spell;
But they ventured to hope that the Snark wouldn't mind
    Undertaking that duty as well.

So the Snark found the verdict, although as it owned,
    It was spent with the toils of the day:
When it said the word, 'GUILTY!' the jury all groaned,
    And some of them fainted away.

Then the Snark pronounced sentence, the Judge being quite
    Too nervous to utter a word:
When it rose to its feet, there was silence like night,
    And the fall of a pin might be heard.

'Transportation for life' was the sentence it gave,
    'And then to be fined forty pound.'
The Jury all cheered, though the Judge said he feared
    That the phrase was not legally sound.

But their wild exultation was suddenly checked
    When the jailer informed them, with tears,
Such a sentence would have not the slightest effect,
    As the pig had been dead for some years.

The Judge left the Court, looking deeply disgusted:
　　But the Snark, though a little aghast,
As the lawyer to whom the defence was entrusted,
　　Went bellowing on to the last.

Thus the Barrister dreamed, while the bellowing seemed
　　To grow every moment more clear:
Till he woke to the knell of a furious bell,
　　Which the Bellman rang close at his ear.

FIT THE SEVENTH

The Banker's Fate

They sought it with thimbles, they sought it with care;
　　They pursued it with forks and hope;
They threatened its life with a railway-share:
　　They charmed it with smiles and soap.

And the Banker, inspired with a courage so new
　　It was matter for general remark,
Rushed madly ahead and was lost to their view
　　In his zeal to discover the Snark.

But while he was seeking with thimbles and care,
　　A Bandersnatch swiftly drew nigh
And grabbed at the Banker, who shrieked in despair,
　　For he knew it was useless to fly.

He offered large discount – he offered a cheque
　　(Drawn 'to bearer') for seven-pounds-ten:
But the Bandersnatch merely extended its neck
　　And grabbed at the Banker again.

Without rest or pause – while those frumious jaws
　　Went savagely snapping around –

He skipped and he hopped, and he floundered and flopped,
  Till fainting he fell to the ground.

The Bandersnatch fled as the others appeared:
  Led on by that fear-stricken yell:
And the Bellman remarked, 'It is just as I feared!'
  And solemnly tolled on his bell.

He was black in the face, and they scarcely could trace
  The least likeness to what he had been:
While so great was his fright that his waistcoat turned white —
  A wonderful thing to be seen!

To the horror of all who were present that day,
  He uprose in full evening dress,
And with senseless grimaces endeavoured to say
  What his tongue could no longer express.

Down he sank in a chair — ran his hands through his hair —
  And chanted in mimsiest tones
Words whose utter inanity proved his insanity,
  While he rattled a couple of bones.

'Leave him here to his fate — it is getting so late!'
  The Bellman exclaimed in a fright.
'We have lost half the day. Any further delay,
  And we shan't catch a Snark before night!'

FIT THE EIGHTH

The Vanishing

They sought it with thimbles, they sought it with care;
  They pursued it with forks and hope;
They threatened its life with a railway-share;
  They charmed it with smiles and soap.

They shuddered to think that the chase might fail,
    And the Beaver, excited at last,
Went bounding along on the tip of its tail,
    For the daylight was nearly past.

'There is Thingumbob shouting!' the Bellman said.
    'He is shouting like mad, only hark!
He is waving his hands, he is wagging his head,
    He has certainly found a Snark!'

They gazed in delight, while the Butcher exclaimed
    'He was always a desperate wag!'
They beheld him – their Baker – their hero unnamed –
    On the top of a neighbouring crag,

Erect and sublime, for one moment of time.
    In the next, that wild figure they saw
(As if stung by a spasm) plunge into a chasm,
    While they waited and listened in awe.

'It's a Snark!' was the sound that first came to their ears,
    And seemed almost too good to be true.
Then followed a torrent of laughter and cheers:
    Then the ominous words, 'It's a Boo –'

Then, silence. Some fancied they heard in the air
    A weary and wandering sigh
That sounded like ' – jum!' but the others declare
    It was only a breeze that went by.

They hunted till darkness came on, but they found
    Not a button, or feather, or mark,
By which they could tell that they stood on the ground
    Where the Baker had met with the Snark.

In the midst of the word he was trying to say
In the midst of his laughter and glee,
He had softly and suddenly vanished away –
For the Snark was a Boojum, you see.

LEWIS CARROLL

The Courtship of the Yonghy-Bonghy-Bò

I

On the Coast of Coromandel
Where the early pumpkins blow,
In the middle of the woods
Lived the Yonghy-Bonghy-Bò.
Two old chairs, and half a candle, –
One old jug without a handle, –
These were all his worldly goods:
In the middle of the woods,
These were all the worldly goods,
Of the Yonghy-Bonghy-Bò,
Of the Yonghy-Bonghy-Bò.

2

Once, among the Bong-trees walking
Where the early pumpkins blow,
To a little heap of stones
Came the Yonghy-Bonghy-Bò.
There he heard a Lady talking,
To some milk-white Hens of Dorking, –
"Tis the Lady Jingly Jones!
On that little heap of stones
Sits the Lady Jingly Jones!'
Said the Yonghy-Bonghy-Bò.
Said the Yonghy-Bonghy-Bò.

3

'Lady Jingly! Lady Jingly!
    Sitting where the pumpkins blow,
        Will you come and be my wife?'
    Said the Yonghy-Bonghy-Bò.
'I am tired of living singly, –
On this coast so wild and shingly, –
        I'm a-weary of my life;
        If you'll come and be my wife,
        Quite serene would be my life!' –
    Said the Yonghy-Bonghy-Bò.
    Said the Yonghy-Bonghy-Bò.

4

'On this Coast of Coromandel,
    Shrimps and watercresses grow,
        Prawns are plentiful and cheap,'
    Said the Yonghy-Bonghy-Bò.
'You shall have my chairs and candle,
And my jug without a handle! –
        Gaze upon the rolling deep
        (Fish is plentiful and cheap);
        As the sea, my love is deep!'
    Said the Yonghy-Bonghy-Bò.
    Said the Yonghy-Bonghy-Bò.

5

Lady Jingly answered sadly,
    And her tears began to flow, –
        'Your proposal comes too late,
    Mr Yonghy-Bonghy-Bo!
I would be your wife most gladly!'
(Here she twirled her fingers madly)
        'But in England I've a mate!

Yes! you've asked me far too late,
For in England I've a mate,
Mr Yonghy-Bonghy-Bò!
Mr Yonghy-Bonghy-Bò.

6

'Mr Jones – (his name is Handel, –
Handel Jones, Esquire, & Co.)
Dorking fowls delights to send,
Mr Yonghy-Bonghy-Bò!
Keep, oh! keep your chairs and candle,
And your jug without a handle, –
I can merely be your friend!
– Should my Jones more Dorkings send,
I will give you three, my friend!
Mr Yonghy-Bonghy-Bò!
Mr Yonghy-Bonghy-Bò!

7

'Though you've such a tiny body,
And your head so large doth grow, –
Though your hat may blow away,
Mr Yonghy-Bonghy-Bò!
Though you're such a Hoddy Doddy –
Yet I wish that I could modi–
fy the words I needs must say!
Will you please to go away?
That is all I have to say –
Mr Yonghy-Bonghy-Bò!
Mr Yonghy-Bonghy-Bò!'

8

Down the slippery slopes of Myrtle,
Where the early pumpkins blow,
To the calm and silent sea

Fled the Yonghy-Bonghy-Bò.
There, beyond the Bay of Gurtle,
Lay a large and lively Turtle: —
    'You're the Cove,' he said, 'for me;
    On your back beyond the sea,
    Turtle, you shall carry me!'
Said the Yonghy-Bonghy-Bò,
Said the Yonghy-Bonghy-Bò.

9

Through the silent-roaring ocean
    Did the Turtle swiftly go;
      Holding fast upon his shell
    Rode the Yonghy-Bonghy-Bò.
With a sad primaeval motion
Towards the sunset isles of Boshen
      Still the Turtle bore him well.
    Holding fast upon his shell,
    'Lady Jingly Jones, farewell!'
Sang the Yonghy-Bonghy-Bò,
Sang the Yonghy-Bonghy-Bò.

10

From the Coast of Coromandel,
    Did that Lady never go;
      On that heap of stones she mourns
    For the Yonghy-Bonghy-Bò.
On that Coast of Coromandel,
In his jug without a handle,
      Still she weeps, and daily moans,
      On that little heap of stones
      To her Dorking Hens she moans,
    For the Yonghy-Bonghy-Bò,
    For the Yonghy-Bonghy-Bò.

EDWARD LEAR

Incidents in the Life of my Uncle Arly

O my agèd Uncle Arly!
Sitting on a heap of Barley
   Through the silent hours of night, –
Close beside a leafy thicket: –
On his nose there was a Cricket, –
In his hat a Railway-Ticket; –
   (But his shoes were far too tight).

Long ago, in youth, he squander'd
All his goods away, and wander'd
   To the Tiniskoop-hills afar.
There on golden sunsets blazing,
Every evening found him gazing, –
Singing – 'Orb! you're quite amazing!
   How I wonder what you are!'

Like the ancient Medes and Persians,
Always by his own exertions
   He subsisted on those hills; –
Whiles, – by teaching children spelling, –
Or at times by merely yelling, –
Or at intervals by selling
   'Propter's Nicodemus Pills'

Later, in his morning rambles
He perceived the moving brambles
   Something square and white disclose; –
'Twas a First-class Railway-Ticket;
But, on stooping down to pick it
Off the ground, – a pea-green Cricket
   Settled on my uncle's Nose.

Never – never more, – oh! never,
Did that Cricket leave him ever, –
     Dawn or evening, day or night; –
Clinging as a constant treasure, –
Chirping with a cheerious measure, –
Wholly to my uncle's pleasure, –
     (Though his shoes were far too tight).

So for three-and-forty winters,
Till his shoes were worn to splinters,
     All those hills he wanders o'er, –
Sometimes silent; – sometimes yelling; –
Till he came to Borley-Melling,
Near his old ancestral dwelling: –
     (But his shoes were far too tight).

On a little heap of Barley
Died my agèd Uncle Arly,
     And they buried him one night; –
Close beside the leafy thicket; –
There, – his hat and Railway-Ticket; –
There, – his ever-faithful Cricket; –
     (But his shoes were far too tight).

                              EDWARD LEAR

The Ballad of Charity

It was in a pleasant deepô, sequestered from the rain,
That many weary passengers were waitin' for the train;
Piles of quite expensive baggage, many a gorgeous portmantó,
Ivory-handled umberellas made a most touristic show.

Whereunto there came a person, very humble was his mien,
Who took an observation of the interestin' scene;

Closely scanned the umberellas, watched with joy the mighty
    trunks,
And observed that all the people were securin' Pullman bunks:

Who was followed shortly after by a most unhappy tramp,
Upon whose features poverty had jounced her iron stamp;
And to make a clear impression, as bees sting you while they buzz,
She had hit him rather harder than she generally does.

For he was so awful ragged, and in parts so awful bare,
That the folks were quite repulsioned to behold him begging there;
And instead of drawing currency from out their pocket-books,
They drew themselves asunder with aversionary looks.

Sternly gazed the first newcomer on the unindulgent crowd,
Then in tones that pierced the deepô he solilicussed aloud: —
'I hev trevelled o'er this cont'nent from Quebec to Bogotáw,
But sech a lot of scallawags as these I never saw.

'Ye are wealthy, ye are gifted, ye have house and lands and rent,
Yet unto a suff'rin' mortal ye will not donate a cent;
Ye expend your missionaries to the heathen and the Jew,
But there isn't any heathen that is half as small as you.

'Ye are lucky — ye hev cheque-books and deeposits in the bank,
And ye squanderate your money on the titled folks of rank;
The onyx and the sardonyx upon your garments shine,
And ye drink at every dinner p'rhaps a dollar's wuth of wine.

'Ye are going for the summer to the islands by the sea,
Where it costs four dollars daily — setch is not for setch as me;
Iv'ry-handled umberellas do not come into my plan,
But I kin give a dollar to this suff'rin' fellow-man.

'Hand-bags made of Rooshy leather are not truly at my call,
Yet in the eyes of Mussy I am richer 'en you all,

For I kin give a dollar wher' you dare not stand a dime,
And never miss it nother, nor regret it any time.'

Sayin' this he drew a wallet from the inner of his vest,
And gave the tramp a daddy, which it was his level best;
Other people, havin' heard him, soon to charity inclined —
One giver soon makes twenty if you only get their wind.

The first who gave the dollar led the other one about,
And at every contribution he a-raised a joyful shout,
Exclaimin' how 'twas noble to relieviate distress,
And remarkin' that our duty is our present happiness.

Thirty dollars altogether were collected by the tramp,
When he bid 'em all good evenin' and went out into the damp,
And was followed briefly after by the one who made the speech,
And who showed by good example how to practise as to preach.

Which soon around the corner the couple quickly met,
And the tramp produced the specie for to liquidate his debt;
And the man who did the preachin' took his twenty of the sum,
Which you see that out of thirty left a tenner for the bum.

And the couple passed the summer at Bar Harbor with the rest,
Greatly changed in their appearance and most elegantly dressed.
Any fowl with change of feathers may a brilliant bird become:
And how hard is life for many! oh how sweet it is for some!

C. G. LELAND

Sir Guy the Crusader

SIR GUY was a doughty crusader,
    A muscular knight,
    Ever ready to fight,
A very determined invader,
    And DICKEY DE LION's delight.

LENORE was a Saracen maiden,
  Brunette, statuesque,
  The reverse of grotesque,
Her pa was a bagman from Aden,
  Her mother she played in burlesque.

A coryphée, pretty and loyal,
  In amber and red
  The ballet she led;
Her mother performed at the Royal,
  LENORE at the Saracen's Head.

Of face and of figure majestic,
  She dazzled the cits —
  Ecstaticised pits; —
Her troubles were only domestic,
  But drove her half out of her wits.

Her father incessantly lashed her,
  On water and bread
  She was grudgingly fed;
Whenever her father he thrashed her
  Her mother sat down on her head.

GUY saw her, and loved her, with reason,
  For beauty so bright
  Sent him mad with delight;
He purchased a stall for the season,
  And sat in it every night.

His views were exceedingly proper,
  He wanted to wed,
  So he called at her shed
And saw her progenitor whop her —
  Her mother sit down on her head.

'So pretty,' said he, 'and so trusting!
    You brute of a dad,
    You unprincipled cad,
·Your conduct is really disgusting,
   Come, come, now admit it's too bad!

'You're a turbaned old Turk, and malignant –
    Your daughter LENORE
    I intensely adore,
And I cannot help feeling indignant,
   A fact that I hinted before;

'To see a fond father employing
    A deuce of a knout
    For to bang her about,
To a sensitive lover's annoying.'
   Said the bagman, 'Crusader, get out.'

Says GUY, 'Shall a warrior laden
    With a big spiky knob,
    Sit in peace on his cob
While a beautiful Saracen maiden
   Is whipped by a Saracen snob?

'To London I'll go from my charmer.'
    Which he did, with his loot
    (Seven hats and a flute),
And was nabbed for his Sydenham armour
   At MR BEN-SAMUEL's suit.

SIR GUY he was lodged in the Compter,
    Her pa, in a rage,
    Died (don't know his age),
His daughter, she married the prompter,
   Grew bulky and quitted the stage.

                 SIR W. S. GILBERT

Finnigin to Flannigan

Superintendent was Flannigan;
Boss av the siction wuz Finnigin;
Whiniver the kyars got offen the thrack,
An' muddled up things t' th' divil an' back,
Finnigin writ it to Flannigan,
After the wrick wuz all on ag'in;
      That is, this Finnigin
      Repoorted to Flannigan.

Whin Finnigin furst writ to Flannigan,
He writed tin pages – did Finnigin,
An' he tould jist how the smash occurred;
Full many a tajus blunderin' wurrd
Did Finnigin write to Flannigan
After the cars had gone on ag'in.
      That was how Finnigin
      Repoorted to Flannigan.

Now Flannigan knowed more than Finnigin –
He'd more idjucation, had Flannigan;
An' it wore'm clane an' complately out
To tell what Finnigin writ about
In his writin' to Muster Flannigan.
So he writed back to Finnigin:
      'Don't do sich a sin ag'in;
      Make 'em brief, Finnigin!'

When Finnigin got this from Flannigan,
He blushed rosy rid, did Finnigin;
An' he said: 'I'll gamble a whole month's pa-ay
That it will be minny and minny a da-ay
Befoore Sup'rintindint – that's Flannigan –
Gets a whack at this very same sin ag'in.

From Finnigin to Flannigan
Repoorts won't be long ag'in.'

*

Wan da-ay, on the siction av Finnigin,
On the road sup'rintinded by Flannigan,
A rail giv way on a bit av a curve,
An' some kyars went off as they made the swerve.
'There's nobody hurted', sez Finnigin,
'But repoorts must be made to Flannigan.'
        An' he winked at McGorrigan,
        As married a Finnigin.

He wuz shantyin' thin, wuz Finnigin,
As minny a railroader's been ag'in,
An' the shmoky ol' lamp wuz burnin' bright
In Finnigin's shanty all that night —
Bilin' down his repoort was Finnigin!
An' he writed this here: 'Muster Flannigan:
        Off ag'in, on ag'in,
        Gone ag'in — Finnigin.'

S. W. GILLINAN

Lady Jane

SAPPHICS

Down the green hill-side fro' the castle window
Lady Jane spied Bill Amaranth a workin';
Day by day watched him go about his ample
                    Nursery garden.

Cabbages thriv'd there, wi' a mort o' green-stuff –
Kidney beans, broad beans, onions, tomatoes,
Artichokes, seakale, vegetable marrows,
                          Early potatoes.

Lady Jane cared not very much for all these:
What she cared much for was a glimpse o' Willum
Strippin' his brown arms wi' a view to horti-
                          Cultural effort.

Little guessed Willum, never extra-vain, that
Up the green hill-side, i' the gloomy castle,
Feminine eyes could so delight to view his
                          Noble proportions.

Only one day while, in an innocent mood,
Moppin' his brow ('cos 'twas a trifle sweaty)
With a blue kerchief – lo, he spies a white 'un
                          Coyly responding.

Oh, delightsome Love! Not a jot do *you* care
For the restrictions set on human inter-
course by cold-blooded social refiners;
                          Nor do I, neither.

Day by day, peepin' fro' behind the bean-sticks,
Willum observed that scrap o' white a-wavin',
Till his hot sighs, out-growin' all repression,
                          Busted his weskit.

Lady Jane's guardian was a haughty Peer, who
Clung to old creeds and had a nasty temper;
Can we blame Willum that he hardly cared to
                          Risk a refusal?

Year by year found him busy 'mid the bean-sticks,
Wholly uncertain how on earth to take steps.
Thus for eighteen years he beheld the maiden
     Wave fro' her window.

But the nineteenth spring, i' the Castle post-bag,
Came by book-post Bill's catalogue o' seedlings
Mark'd wi' blue ink at 'Paragraphs relatin'
     Mainly to Pumpkins.'

'W.A. can,' so the Lady Jane read,
'Strongly commend that very noble Gourd, the
Lady Jane, first-class medal, ornamental;
     Grows to a great height.'

Scarce a year arter, by the scented hedgerows –
Down the mown hillside, fro' the castle gateway –
Came a long train and, i' the midst, a black bier,
     Easily shouldered.

'Whose is yon corse that, thus adorned wi' gourd-leaves,
Forth ye bear with slow step?' A mourner answer'd,
''Tis the poor clay-cold body Lady Jane grew
     Tired to abide in.'

'Delve my grave quick, then, for I die tomorrow.
Delve it one furlong fro' the kidney bean-sticks,
Where I may dream she's goin' on precisely
     As she was used to.'

Hardly died Bill when, fro' the Lady Jane's grave,
Crept to his white death-bed a lovely pumpkin:
Clim' the house-wall and over-arched his head wi'
     Billowy verdure.

Simple this tale! – but delicately perfumed
As the sweet roadside honeysuckle. That's why,
Difficult though it's metre was to tackle,
              I'm glad I wrote it.

                              SIR A. QUILLER-COUCH

Rebecca

WHO SLAMMED DOORS FOR FUN AND PERISHED MISERABLY

A Trick that everyone abhors
In Little Girls is slamming Doors
A
     Wealthy Banker's
               Little Daughter
          Who lived in Palace Green, Bayswater
          (by name Rebecca Offendort)
          Was given to this Furious Sport.
She would deliberately go
And slam the door like
               Billy-Ho!
     To make
          her
                    Uncle Jacob start.
She was not really bad at heart,
But only rather rude and wild:
She was an aggravating child. . . .

It happened that a Marble Bust
Of Abraham was standing just
Above the Door this little Lamb
Had carefully prepared to Slam,
And Down it came! It knocked her flat!
It laid her out! She looked
               like that.

Her funeral Sermon (which was long
And followed by a Sacred Song)
Mentioned her Virtues, it is true,
But dwelt upon her Vices too,
And showed the Dreadful End of One
Who goes and slams the door for Fun.

*

The children who were brought to hear
The awful Tale from far and near
Were much impressed,
                    and inly swore
They never more would slam the Door.
— As often they had done before.

HILAIRE BELLOC

Charles Augustus Fortescue,

WHO ALWAYS DID WHAT WAS RIGHT, AND SO
ACCUMULATED AN IMMENSE FORTUNE

The nicest child I ever knew
Was Charles Augustus Fortescue.
He never lost his cap, or tore
His stockings or his pinafore:
    In eating Bread he made no Crumbs,
    He was extremely fond of sums,

To which, however, he preferred
The Parsing of a Latin Word —
He sought, when it was in his power,
For information twice an hour,
And as for finding Mutton-Fat
Unappetising, far from that!

He often, at his Father's Board,
Would beg them, of his own accord,
To give him, if they did not mind,
The Greasiest Morsels they could find —
His later years did not belie
The Promise of his Infancy.
In Public Life he always tried
To take a judgement Broad and Wide;
In Private, none was more than he
Renowned for quiet courtesy.
He rose at once in his Career,
And long before his Fortieth Year
Had wedded
Fifi,
   Only Child
Of Bunyan, First Lord Aberfylde,
He thus became immensely Rich,
And built the Spendid Mansion which
Is called
'The Cedars,
  Muswell Hill.'
Where he resides in Affluence still
To show what Everybody might
Become by
  SIMPLY DOING RIGHT.

      HILAIRE BELLOC

The Bath

Broad is the Gate and wide the Path
That leads man to his daily bath;
But ere you spend the shining hour
With plunge and spray, with sluice and show'r —

With all that teaches you to dread
The bath as little as your bed –
Remember, wheresoe'er you be,
To shut the door and turn the key!

I had a friend – my friend no more! –
Who failed to bolt the bath-room door;

A maiden-aunt of his, one day,
Walked in, as half-submerged he lay!

But did not notice nephew John,
And turned the boiling water on!

He had no time, or even scope,
To camouflage himself with soap,
But gave a yell and flung aside
The sponge, 'neath which he sought to hide!

It fell to earth I know not where!
He beat his breast in his despair,

And then, like Venus from the foam,
Sprang into view, and made for home!

His aunt fell fainting to the ground!
Alas! They never brought her round!

She died, intestate, in her prime,
The victim of another's crime;

And John can never quite forget
How, by a breach of etiquette,
He lost, at one fell swoop (or plunge)
His aunt, his honour, and his sponge!

HARRY GRAHAM

Dangerous Establishment

My favourite café – so I dreamed recently –
Stood amidst palm-trees in an island port.
Now, Margate is *my* holiday resort;
But dreams are rather apt to cross the sea.

I settled near the window, ill at ease:
Where once the number 2 bus used to stop
They'd set a kind of pristine jungle up
And apes – orang-outangs – hung on the trees.

I'm sure they'd not been there so very long:
You can't just change dimensions, yards and feet.
Before I came it was still Bishop Street;
You pick a place, and now it's Belitong.

At first I felt like asking the head waiter.
But then I thought this wasn't any good.
What sort of comment should a man called Slater
Make on this business, even if he could?

Now the door opened. It was Dr Clare.
And, close behind him, a black panther who
Sat down as any Tom or Dick might do –
And at my table, on a vacant chair.

I asked him softly if he'd care to smoke.
He did not stir, but stared at me defiant.
Now the proprietor approached this client,
Solemnly tickled him, but never spoke.

The waiter brought us scrambled egg on toast.
He walked on tip-toe and seemed liverish.
The panther did not touch this wholesome dish
But ate poor Slater. Peace be with his ghost!

From up above came sounds of ball and cue.
The panther dined. He saw no need to hurry.
What could I do but sit there, watch and worry,
With jungle all around, no number 2?

Because they called me to the phone (old Deeping,
My senior clerk, to tell me he was sick).
I was obliged to make my exit quick.
When I came back I saw that I was sleeping.

ERICH KÄSTNER
(translated by MICHAEL HAMBURGER)

Repeat Performance

'False, false!' young Richard cried, and threw the stone
    Into the lake, and gave her in its stead
A single rose. Pacing the shore alone,
    'Deceived, deceived!' he cried: which done and said,
    He put the pistol up against his head
And, though he wasn't very good at gunnery,
    Could hardly miss. As soon as he was dead
Fair Isabel retired into a nunnery.

*

So ends my tale. In case you came in late,
    Where, when and why these various things were done,
    Whether the stone was his, or hers as well,
    And whether *it* was false or Isabel,
    And why he died and she became a nun,
I will recall and in due course relate.

P. M. HUBBARD

SQUINTS AT NATURE

The Filbert

Nay, gather not that Filbert, Nicholas,
There is a maggot there ... it is his house, ...
His castle, ... oh commit not burglary!
Strip him not naked, ... 'tis his clothes, his shell,
His bones, the case and armour of his life,
And thou shalt do no murder, Nicholas!
It were an easy thing to crack that nut
Or with thy crackers or thy double teeth,
So easily may all things be destroy'd!
But 'tis not in the power of mortal man
To mend the fracture of a filbert shell.
There were two great men once amused themselves
Watching two maggots run their wriggling race,
And wagering on their speed; but Nick, to us
It were no sport to see the pamper'd worm
Roll out and then draw in his rolls of fat,
Like to some Barber's leathern powder-bag
Wherewith he feathers, frosts, or cauliflowers
Spruce Beau, or Lady fair, or Doctor grave.
Enough of dangers and of enemies
Hath Nature's wisdom for the worm ordain'd,
Increase not thou the number! Him the Mouse,
Gnawing with nibbling tooth the shell's defence,
May from his native tenement eject;
Him may the Nut-hatch, piercing with strong bill,
Unwittingly destroy; or to his hoard
The Squirrel bear, at leisure to be crack'd.
Man also hath his dangers and his foes
As this poor Maggot hath; and when I muse
Upon the aches, anxieties, and fears,
The Maggot knows not, Nicholas, methinks
It were a happy metamorphosis
To be enkernell'd thus: never to hear

Of wars, and of invasions, and of plots,
Kings, Jacobins, and Tax-commissioners;
To feel no motion but the wind that shook
The Filbert Tree, and rock'd us to our rest;
And in the middle of such exquisite food
To live luxurious! The perfection this
Of snugness! it were to unite at once
Hermit retirement, Aldermanic bliss,
And Stoic independence of mankind.

ROBERT SOUTHEY

To a Fish

You strange, astonished-looking, angle-faced,
    Dreary-mouthed, gaping wretches of the sea,
    Gulping salt-water everlastingly,
Cold-blooded, though with red your blood be graced,
And mute, though dwellers in the roaring waste;
    And you, all shapes beside, that fishy be, –
    Some round, some flat, some long, all devilry,
Legless, unloving, infamously chaste; –

O scaly, slippery, wet, swift, staring wights,
    What is't ye do? What life lead? eh, dull goggles?
How do ye vary your vile days and nights?
    How pass your Sundays? Are ye still but joggles
In ceaseless wash? Still nought but gapes, and bites,
    And drinks, and stares, diversified with boggles?

A Fish Answers

Amazing monster! that, for aught I know,
    With the first sight of thee didst make our race
    For ever stare! O flat and shocking face,
Grimly divided from the breast below!

Thou that on dry land horribly dost go
   With a split body and most ridiculous pace,
   Prong after prong, disgracer of all grace,
Long-useless-finned, haired, upright, unwet, slow!
O breather of unbreathable, sword-sharp air,
   How canst exist? How bear thyself, thou dry
And dreary sloth? What particle canst share
   Of the only blessed life, the watery?
I sometimes see of ye an actual *pair*
   Go by! linked fin by fin! most odiously.

                        LEIGH HUNT

How doth the little......

How doth the little crocodile
   Improve his shining tail,
And pour the waters of the Nile
   On every golden scale!

How cheerfully he seems to grin,
   How neatly spreads his claws,
And welcomes little fishes in,
   With gently smiling jaws!

                    LEWIS CARROLL

The Walrus and the Carpenter

The sun was shining on the sea,
   Shining with all his might:
He did his very best to make
   The billows smooth and bright —
And this was odd, because it was
   The middle of the night.

The moon was shining sulkily,
  Because she thought the sun
Had got no business to be there
  After the day was done –
'It's very rude of him,' she said,
  'To come and spoil the fun!'

The sea was wet as wet could be,
  The sands were dry as dry.
You could not see a cloud, because
  No cloud was in the sky:
No birds were flying overhead –
  There were no birds to fly.

The Walrus and the Carpenter
  Were walking close at hand:
They wept like anything to see
  Such quantities of sand:
'If this were only cleared away,'
  They said, 'it would be grand!'

'If seven maids with seven mops
  Swept it for half a year,
Do you suppose,' the Walrus said,
  'That they could get it clear?'
'I doubt it,' said the Carpenter,
  And shed a bitter tear.

'O Oysters, come and walk with us!'
  The Walrus did beseech.
'A pleasant walk, a pleasant talk,
  Along the briny beach:
We cannot do with more than four,
  To give a hand to each.'

The eldest Oyster looked at him,
  But never a word he said:

The eldest Oyster winked his eye,
    And shook his heavy head –
Meaning to say he did not choose
    To leave the oyster-bed.

But four young Oysters hurried up,
    All eager for the treat:
Their coats were brushed, their faces washed,
    Their shoes were clean and neat –
And this was odd, because you know,
    They hadn't any feet.

Four other Oysters followed them,
    And yet another four;
And thick and fast they came at last,
    And more, and more, and more –
All hopping through the frothy waves,
    And scrambling to the shore.

The Walrus and the Carpenter
    Walked on a mile or so,
And then they rested on a rock
    Conveniently low:
And all the little Oysters stood
    And waited in a row.

'The time has come,' the Walrus said,
    'To talk of many things:
Of shoes – and ships – and sealing wax –
    Of cabbages – and kings –
And why the sea is boiling hot –
    And whether pigs have wings.'

'But wait a bit,' the Oysters cried,
    'Before we have our chat;
For some of us are out of breath,
    And all of us are fat!'

'No hurry!' said the Carpenter.
    They thanked him much for that.

'A loaf of bread,' the Walrus said,
    'Is what we chiefly need:
Pepper and vinegar besides
    Are very good indeed –
Now, if you're ready, Oysters dear,
    We can begin to feed.'

'But not on us!' the Oysters cried,
    Turning a little blue.
'After such kindness, that would be
    A dismal thing to do!'
'The night is fine,' the Walrus said,
    'Do you admire the view?

'It was so kind of you to come!
    And you are very nice!'
The Carpenter said nothing but
    'Cut us another slice.
I wish you were not quite so deaf –
    I've had to ask you twice!'

'It seems a shame,' the Walrus said,
    'To play them such a trick.
After we've brought them out so far,
    And made them trot so quick!'
The Carpenter said nothing but
    'The butter's spread too thick!'

'I weep for you,' the Walrus said:
    'I deeply sympathize.'
With sobs and tears he sorted out
    Those of the largest size,

Holding his pocket-handkerchief
  Before his streaming eyes.

'O Oysters,' said the Carpenter,
  'You've had a pleasant run!
Shall we be trotting home again!'
  But answer came there none –
And this was scarcely odd, because
  They'd eaten every one.

LEWIS CARROLL

The Lobster-Quadrille

'Will you walk a little faster?' said a whiting to a snail,
'There's a porpoise close behind us, and he's treading on my tail.
See how eagerly the lobsters and the turtles all advance!
They are waiting on the shingle – will you come and join the dance?
Will you, won't you, will you, won't you, will you join the dance?
Will you, won't you, will you, won't you, won't you join the
    dance?

'You can really have no notion how delightful it will be
When they take us up and throw us, with the lobsters, out to sea!'
But the snail replied 'Too far, too far!' and gave a look askance –
Said he thanked the whiting kindly, but he would not join the
    dance.
    Would not, could not, would not, could not, could
      not join the dance.
    Would not, could not, would not, could not, could
      not join the dance.

'What matters it how far we go?' his scaly friend replied.
'There is another shore, you know, upon the other side.
The further off from England, the nearer is to France.

Then turn not pale, beloved snail, but come and join the dance.
    Will you, won't you, will you, won't you, will you
       join the dance?
    Will you, won't you, will you, won't you, will you
       join the dance?'

LEWIS CARROLL

I passed by his garden ...

I passed by his garden, and marked with one eye,
How the Owl and the Panther were sharing a pie:
The Panther took pie-crust, and gravy, and meat,
While the Owl had the dish as its share of the treat.
When the pie was all finished, the Owl, as a boon,
Was kindly permitted to pocket the spoon:
While the Panther received knife and fork with a growl,
And concluded the banquet by –

LEWIS CARROLL

A Sea Dirge

There are certain things – a spider, a ghost,
    The income-tax, gout, an umbrella for three –
That I hate, but the thing that I hate the most
    Is a thing they call the SEA.

Pour some cold water over the floor –
    Ugly I'm sure you'll allow it to be:
Suppose it extended a mile or more,
    That's very like the SEA.

Beat a dog till it howls outright –
    Cruel, but all very well for a spree:
Suppose that one did so day and night,
    That would be like the SEA.

I had a vision of nursery-maids;
   Tens of thousands passed by me –
All leading children with wooden spades,
   And this was by the SEA.

Who invented those spades of wood?
   Who was it cut them out of the tree?
None, I think, but an idiot could –
   Or one that loved the SEA.

It is pleasant and dreamy, no doubt, to float
   With 'thoughts as boundless, and souls as free';
But suppose you are very unwell in a boat,
   How do you like the SEA?

There is an insect that people avoid
   (Whence is derived the verb 'to flee')
Where have you been by it most annoyed?
   In lodgings by the SEA.

If you like coffee with sand for dregs,
   A decided hint of salt in your tea,
And a fishy taste in the very eggs –
   By all means choose the SEA.

And if, with these dainties to drink and eat,
   You prefer not a vestige of grass or tree,
And a chronic state of wet in your feet,
   Then – I recommend the SEA.

For *I* have friends who dwell by the coast,
   Pleasant friends they are to me!
It is when I'm with them I wonder most
   That anyone likes the SEA.

They take me a walk: though tired and stiff,
   To climb the heights I madly agree:

And, after a tumble or so from the cliff,
    They kindly suggest the SEA.

I try the rocks, and I think it cool
    That they laugh with such an excess of glee,
As I heavily slip into every pool
    That skirts the cold, cold SEA.

                                        LEWIS CARROLL

The Pelican Chorus

King and Queen of the Pelicans we;
No other birds so grand as we!
None but we have feet like fins!
With lovely leathery throats and chins!
        Ploffskin, Pluffskin, Pelican jee!
        We think no birds so happy as we!
        Plumpskin, Ploshkin, Pelican Jill!
        We think so then, and we thought so still!

We live on the Nile. The Nile we love.
By night we sleep on the cliffs above.
By day we fish, and at eve we stand
On long bare islands of yellow sand.
And when the sun sinks slowly down
And the great rock walls grow dark and brown,
Where the purple river rolls fast and dim
And the ivory Ibis starlike skim,
Wing to wing we dance around, –
Stamping our feet with a flumpy sound, –
Opening our mouths as Pelicans ought,
And this is the song we nightly snort
        Ploffskin, etc. (as before).

Last year came out our Daughter, Dell;
And all the birds received her well.
To do her honour, a feast we made
For every bird that can swim or wade.
Herons and Gulls, and Cormorants black,
Cranes, and Flamingoes with scarlet back,
Plovers and Storks, and Geese in crowds.
Thousands of Birds in wondrous flight!
They ate and drank and danced all night,
And echoing back from the rocks you heard
Multitude-echoes from Bird and Bird, –
      Ploffskin, etc. (*as before*).

Yes, they came; and among the rest,
The King of the Cranes all grandly dressed.
Such a lovely tail! Its feathers float
Between the ends of his blue dress-coat;
With pea-green trowsers all so neat,
And a delicate frill to hide his feet, –
(For though no one speaks of it, everyone knows,
He had got no webs between his toes!)
As soon as he saw our Daughter Dell,
In violent love that Crane King fell, –
On seeing her waddling form so fair,
With a wreath of shrimps in her short white hair,
And before the end of the next long day,
Our Dell had given her heart away;
For the King of the Cranes had won that heart,
With a Crocodile's egg and a large fish-tart.
She vowed to marry the King of the Cranes,
Leaving the Nile for stranger plains;
And away they flew in a lengthening cloud.
      Ploffskin, etc. (*as before*).

And far away in the twilight sky,
We heard them singing a lessening cry, –

Farther and farther till out of sight,
And we stood alone in the silent night!
Often since, in the nights of June,
We sit on the sand and watch the moon; —
She has gone to the great Gromboolian plain,
And we probably never shall meet again!
Oft, in the long still nights of June,
We sit on the rocks and watch the moon; —
— She dwells by the streams of the Chankly Bore,
And we probably never shall meet her more.
      Ploffskin, etc. (*as before*).

EDWARD LEAR

The Irish Pig

'Twas an evening in November,
As I very well remember,
I was strolling down the street in drunken pride,
But my knees were all aflutter,
So I landed in the gutter,
And a pig came up and lay down by my side.

Yes, I lay there in the gutter
Thinking thoughts I could not utter,
When a colleen passing by did softly say,
'Ye can tell a man that boozes
By the company he chooses.' —
At that the pig got up and walked away!

ANON.

Ah, Who?

Who comes so damp by grass and grave
    At ghastly twilight hour,
And bubbles forth his pois'nous breath
    On ev'ry shudd'ring flow'r?

Who dogs the houseless wanderer
 Upon the wintry wold;
And kisses – with his frothy lips –
 The clammy brow and cold?

Who, hideous, trails a slimy form
 Betwixt the moonlight pale,
And the pale, fearful, sleeping face?
 Our little friend – the Snail.

H. CHOLMONDELEY-PENNELL

The Frog

Be kind and tender to the Frog,
 And do not call him names,
As 'Slimy skin', or 'Polly-wog',
 Or likewise 'Ugly James',
Or 'Gap-a-grin', or 'Toad-gone-wrong',
 Or 'Billy Bandy-knees':
The Frog is justly sensitive
 To epithets like these.
No animal will more repay
 A treatment kind and fair;
At least so lonely people say
Who keep a frog (and, by the way,
They are extremely rare).

HILAIRE BELLOC

The Python

A Python I should not advise, –
It needs a doctor for its eyes,
And has the measles yearly.
However, if you feel inclined
To get one (to improve your mind,

And not for fashion merely),
Allow no music near its cage;
And when it flies into a rage
Chastise it, most severely.

I had an aunt in Yucatan
Who bought a Python from a man
   And kept it for a pet.
She died, because she never knew
These simple little rules and few; —
   The snake is living yet.

HILAIRE BELLOC

D

The Dreadful Dinotherium he
Will have to do his best for D.
The early world observed with awe
His back, indented like a saw.
His look was gay, his voice was strong;
His tail was neither short nor long;
His trunk, or elongated nose,
Was not so large as some suppose;
His teeth, as all the world allows,
Were graminivorous, like a cow's.
He therefore should have wished to pass
Long peaceful nights upon the Grass,
But, being mad, the brute preferred
To roost in branches, like a bird.[1]
A creature heavier than a whale,
You see at once, could hardly fail
To suffer badly when he slid
And tumbled (as he always did).

   1. We have good reason to suppose
      He did so, from his claw-like toes.

His fossil, therefore, comes to light
All broken up: and serve him right.

MORAL

If you were born to walk the ground,
Remain there; do not fool around.

HILAIRE BELLOC

The Pretender

In the greens of the wilds of Seringapatam
Is the haunt of an ancient redoubtable ram,
  With sharp-pointed horns on its head;
When it snuffs out a Brahmin it scoops with its hooves,
Till the jungle around it is jungle in grooves,
  And then it pretends to be dead.

O White Man, beware of such tactics as these,
For if in compassion thou sink to thy knees,
  All thought of mere safety forgot,
With a jerk of its horns the fell creature comes to,
And smiles, as if saying, 'Ah, friend, is it you?'
  When there's none to reply, 'It is not'.

WALTER DE LA MARE

Lines on Montezuma

MEXICAN LEGEND

by a Passman

Montezuma
Met a puma
Coming through the rye:
Montezuma made the puma
Into apple pie.

Invitation
To the nation
Everyone to come.
Montezuma
And the puma
Give a kettle-drum.

Acceptation
Of the nation
One and all invited.
Montezuma –
And the puma
Equally delighted.

Preparation,
Ostentation,
Dresses rich prepared:
Feathers – jewels –
Work in crewels –
No expenses spared.

Congregation
Of the nation
Round the palace wall.
Awful rumour
That the puma
Won't be served to all,

Deputation
From the nation,
Audience they gain
'What's this rumour?
Montezuma,
If you please, explain.'

Montezuma
(Playful humour

very well sustained)
Answers: 'Piedish
As it's my dish,
Is for me retained.'

Exclamation!
Indignation!
Feeling running high.
Montezuma
Joins the puma
In the apple pie.

D. F. ALDERSON

The Legend of the First Cam-u-el

AN ARABIAN APOLOGUE

Across the sands of Syria,
Or, possibly, Algeria,
Or some benighted neighbourhood of barrenness and drouth,
There came the prophet Sam-u-el
Upon the only Cam-u-el –
A bumpy, grumpy Quadruped of discontented mouth.

The atmosphere was glutinous;
The Cam-u-el was mutinous;
He dumped the pack from off his back; with horrid grunts and
squeals
He made the desert hideous;
With strategy perfidious
He tied his neck in curlicues, he kicked his paddy heels.

Then quoth the gentle Sam-u-el,
'You rogue, I ought to lam you well!
Though zealously I've shielded you from every grief and woe,

It seems, to voice a platitude,
You haven't any gratitude.
I'd like to know what cause you have for doing thus and so!'

To him replied the Cam-u-el,
'I beg your pardon, Sam-u-el.
I know that I'm a Reprobate, I know that I'm a Freak;
But oh! this utter loneliness!
My too distinguished Onliness!
Were there but other Cam-u-els I wouldn't be Unique.'

The Prophet beamed beguilingly.
'Aha', he answered smilingly,
'You feel the need of company? I clearly understand.
We'll speedily create for you
The corresponding mate for you —
Ho! presto, change-o, dinglebat!' — he waved a potent hand,

And, lo! from out Vacuity
A second Incongruity,
To wit, a Lady Cam-u-el was born through magic art.
Her structure anatomical,
Her form and face were comical;
She was, in short, a Cam-u-el, the other's counterpart.

As Spaniards gaze on Aragon,
Upon that Female Paragon
So gazed the Prophet's Cam-u-el, that primal Desert Ship.
A connoisseur meticulous,
He found her that ridiculous
He grinned from ear to auricle *until he split his lip!*

Because of his temerity
That Cam-u-el's posterity
Must wear divided upper lips through all their solemn lives!
A prodigy astonishing
Reproachfully admonishing
Those wicked, heartless married men who ridicule their wives.

ARTHUR GUITERMAN

The Shakespearean Bear

(THE WINTER'S TALE, *Act III, Scene 3*)

When, on our casual way,
    Troubles and dangers accrue
Till there's the devil to pay,
    How shall we carry it through?
    Shakespeare, that oracle true,
Teacher in doubt and despair.
    Told us the best that he knew:
'Exit, pursued by a bear'.

That is the line of a play
    Dear to the cognizant few;
Hark to its lilt, and obey!
    Constantly keep it in view.
    Fate, the malevolent shrew,
Weaves her implacable snare;
    What is a fellow to do?
'Exit, pursued by a bear.'

Take to your heels while you may!
    Sinister tabby-cats mew,
Witches that scheme to betray
    Mingle their horrible brew,
    Thunderclouds darken the blue,
Beelzebub growls from his lair;
    Maybe he's hunting for *you!*–
'Exit, pursued by a bear.'

ENVOI

Bores of the dreariest hue,
    Bringers of worry and care,
Watch us respond to our cue, –
    'Exit, pursued by a bear.'

ARTHUR GUITERMAN

Skimbleshanks: The Railway Cat

There's a whisper down the line at 11.39
When the Night Mail's ready to depart,
Saying 'Skimble where is Skimble has he gone to hunt the thimble?
We must find him or the train can't start.'
All the guards and all the porters and the stationmaster's daughters
They are searching high and low,
Saying, 'Skimble where is Skimble for unless he's very nimble
Then the Night Mail just can't go.'
At 11.42 then the signal's nearly due
And the passengers are frantic to a man —
Then Skimble will appear and he'll saunter to the rear:
He's been busy in the luggage van!
    He gives one flash of his glass-green eyes
        And the signal goes 'All Clear!'
    And we're off at last for the northern part
        Of the Northern Hemisphere.

You may say that by and large it is Skimble who's in charge
Of the Sleeping Car Express.
From the driver and the guards to the bagmen playing cards
He will supervise them all, more or less.
Down the corridor he paces and examines all the faces
Of the travellers in the First and in the Third;
He establishes control by a regular patrol
And he'd know at once if anything occurred.
He will watch you without winking and he sees what you are
        thinking
And it's certain that he doesn't approve
Of hilarity and riot, so the folk are very quiet
When Skimble is about and on the move.
    You can play no pranks with Skimbleshanks!
        He's a Cat that cannot be ignored;
    So nothing goes wrong on the Northern Mail
        When Skimbleshanks is aboard.

Oh it's very pleasant when you've found your little den
With your name written up on the door.
And the berth is very neat with a newly folded sheet
And there's not a speck of dust on the floor.
There is every sort of light — you can make it dark or bright;
There's a handle that you turn to make a breeze.
There's a funny little basin you're supposed to wash your face in
And a crank to shut the window if you sneeze.
Then the guard looks in politely and will ask you very brightly
'Do you like your morning tea weak or strong?'
But Skimble's just behind him and was ready to remind him,
For Skimble won't let anything go wrong.
   And when you creep into your cosy berth
      And pull up the counterpane,
    You ought to reflect that it's very nice
      To know that you won't be bothered by mice —
   You can leave all that to the Railway Cat,
     The Cat of the Railway Train!

In the watches of the night he is always fresh and bright;
Every now and then he has a cup of tea
With perhaps a drop of Scotch while he's keeping on the watch,
Only stopping here and there to catch a flea.
You were fast asleep at Crewe and so you never knew
That he was walking up and down the station;
You were sleeping all the while he was busy at Carlisle,
Where he greets the stationmaster with elation.
But you saw him at Dumfries, where he speaks to the police
If there's anything they ought to know about:
When you get to Gallowgate there you do not have to wait —
For Skimbleshanks will help you to get out!
   He gives you a wave of his long brown tail
     Which says: 'I'll see you again!
   You'll meet without fail on the Midnight Mail
    The Cat of the Railway Train.'

T. S. ELIOT

Lullaby for Jumbo

Jumbo asleep!
Grey leaves, thick-furred
As his ears, keep
Conversations blurred.
Thicker than hide
Is the trumpeting water;
Don Pasquito's bride
And his youngest daughter
Watch the leaves
Elephantine grey:
What is it grieves
In the torrid day?
Is it the animal
World that snores
Harsh and inimical
In sleepy pores? –
And why should the spined flowers
Red as a soldier
Make Don Pasquito
Seem still mouldier?

DAME EDITH SITWELL

Do You Know?

'No!' said the Carrot, 'it's not like that.
It's broader, and lighter, and not so fat.
It's never been known to raise its hat –
But it likes to swim in the sea.

'It peers through the night with its pale-green eyes
Which revolve in their sockets contrariwise,
And when it's happy it merely sighs
Wherever it happens to be.

'It loves to dance as it sings a song
With the words half right and the tune all wrong
To the sound of a curious high-pitched gong
In the shade of the banyan tree.

'It frequently tries to touch its toes,
It makes strange noises, wherever it goes,
But *why* it does – well, nobody knows
Excepting the Sphinx and me.'

ALAN CRICK

The Diplomatic Platypus

I had a duck-billed platypus when I was up at Trinity,
With whom I soon discovered a remarkable affinity.
He used to live in lodgings with myself and Arthur Purvis,
And we all went up together for the Diplomatic Service.
I had a certain confidence, I own, in his ability,
He mastered all the subjects with remarkable facility;
And Purvis, though more dubious, agreed that he was clever,
But no one else imagined he had any chance whatever.
I failed to pass the interview, the Board with wry grimaces
Took exception to my boots and then objected to my braces,
And Purvis too was failed by an intolerant examiner
Who said he had his doubts as to his sock-suspenders' stamina.
The bitterness of failure was considerably mollified,
However, by the ease with which our platypus had qualified.
The wisdom of the choice, it soon appeared, was undeniable;
There never was a diplomat more thoroughly reliable.
He never made rash statements his enemies might hold him to,
He never stated anything, for no one ever told him to,
And soon he was appointed, so correct was his behaviour,
Our Minister (without Portfolio) to Trans-Moravia.
My friend was loved and honoured from the Andes to Esthonia,
He soon achieved a pact between Peru and Patagonia,

He never vexed the Russians nor offended the Rumanians,
He pacified the Letts and yet appeased the Lithuanians,
Won approval from his masters down in Downing Street so wholly, O,
He was soon to be rewarded with the grant of a Portfolio,

When, on the Anniversary of Greek Emancipation,
Alas! He laid an egg in the Bulgarian Legation.
This untoward occurrence caused unheard-of repercussions,
Giving rise to epidemics of sword-clanking in the Prussians.
The Poles began to threaten, and the Finns began to flap at him,
Directing all the blame for this unfortunate mishap at him;
While the Swedes withdrew entirely from the Anglo-Saxon dailies
The right of photographing the Aurora Borealis,
And, all efforts at rapprochement in the meantime proving barren,
The Japanese in self-defence annexed the Isle of Arran.
My platypus, once thought to be more cautious and more tentative
Than any other living diplomatic representative,
Was now a sort of warning to all diplomatic students
Of the risks attached to negligence, the perils of imprudence,
And, branded in the Honours List as 'Platypus, Dame Vera',
Retired, a lonely figure, to lay eggs at Bordighera.

PATRICK BARRINGTON

Our Pond

I am fond
Of our pond,
Of the superfine gloss
On its moss,
Its pink lilies and things
And the wings
    Of its duck.

I am keen
On the green
Soupy surface of some
Of its scum,
Its water-waved weeds,
Its three reeds
    And its muck.

Yesterday,
As I lay
And admired its thick skin,
I fell in;
I went walloping down
Till I stuck.

I am fond
Of our pond,
But I like it much more
From the shore.
It was quite out of place
On my face,
    Where it stuck.

DANIEL PETTIWARD

The Sensible Sea-Lion

The sea-lion, naturalists disclose,
Can balance balls upon his nose,
And some, so neatly does he judge it,
Ask, 'If a ball, why not a budget?'
No head for figures is his knob –
His eye's not on the Chancellor's job.
He doesn't balance gains with losses,
But pleasure on his own proboscis.
And rightly, he prefers to win his
Spurs by demonstrating Guinness.

Perhaps this very session he'll
Be chosen as Lord Privy Seal.

J. G. C. TRENCH

London Tom-Cat

Look at the gentle savage, monstrous gentleman
With jungles in his heart, yet metropolitan
As we shall never be; who – while his human hosts,
Afraid of their own past and its primaeval ghosts,
Pile up great walls for comfort – walks coquettishly
Through their elaborate cares, sure of himself and free
To be like them, domesticated, or aloof!
A dandy in the room, a demon on the roof,
He's delicately tough, endearingly reserved,
Adaptable, fastidious, rope-and-fibre-nerved.
Now an accomplished Yogi good at sitting still
He ponders ancient mysteries on the window-sill,
Now stretches, bares his claws and saunters off to find
The thrills of love and hunting, cunningly combined.
Acrobat, diplomat, and simple tabby cat,
He conjures tangled forests in a furnished flat.

MICHAEL HAMBURGER

The Canary

The song of canaries
Never varies,
And when they're moulting
They're pretty revolting.

OGDEN NASH

TRICKS AND TEASES

My Lady went to Canterbury

My heart of gold as true as steel,
As I me leaned to a bough,
In faith but if ye love me well,
Lord, so Robin lough?

My lady went to Canterbury,
   The saint to be her boot;
She met with Kate of Malmesbury:
   Why sleepest thou in an apple root?

Nine mile to Michaelmas,
   Our dame began to brew;
Michael set his mare to grass,
   Lord, so fast it snew!

For you, love, I brake my glass,
   Your gown is furred with blue:
The devil is dead, for there I was;
   Iwis it is full true.

And if ye sleep, the cock will crow,
   True heart, think what I say;
Jackanapes will make a mow,
   Look, who dare say him nay?

I pray you have me now in mind,
   I tell you of the matter;
He blew his horn against the wind;
   The crow goeth to the water.

Yet I tell you mickle more:
   The cat lieth in the cradle;
I pray you keep true heart in store;
   A penny for a ladle.

I swear by Saint Katherine of Kent,
    The goose goeth to the green;
All our dogges tails is brent,
    It is not as I ween.

Tirlery lorpin, the laverock sang,
    So merrily pipes the sparrow,
The cow brake loose, the rope ran home,
    Sir, God give you good morrow!

ANON.

A Non-Sequitur

Marke how the lanterns cloud mine eyes
See where a moone-drake ginnes to rise
Saturne craules much like an *Iron Catt*
To see the naked moone in a slippshott hatt
Thunder thumping toad stooles crock the pots
        To see the meremaids tumble
Leather catt-a-mountaines shake their heeles
        To hear the gosh-hawke grumble
            The rustie thread
            Begins to bleede
        And cobwebs elbows itches
            The putrid skies
            Eat mulsacke pies
        Backed up in logick breeches
Munday trenchers make good hay
The lobster wears no dagger
Meal-mouth'd shee-peacockes powle the starres
And make the lowbell stagger
        Blew crocodiles foame in the toe
        Blind meal-bagges do follow the doe
A ribb of apple braine spice
Will follow the Lancasheire dice

Hark how the chime of Pluto's pispot cracks
To see the rainbowes wheele ganne, made of flax.

RICHARD CORBET

Nottamun Town

In Nottamun Town not a soul would look up,
Not a soul would look up, not a soul would look down,
Not a soul would look up, not a soul would look down
To tell me the way to Nottamun Town.

I rode a big horse that was called a grey mare,
Grey mane and tail, grey stripes down his back,
Grey mane and tail, grey stripes down his back,
There weren't a hair on him but what was called black.

She stood so still, she threw me to the dirt,
She tore my hide and bruised my shirt;
From stirrup to stirrup, I mounted again
And on my ten toes I rode over the plain

Met the King and the Queen and a company of men
A-walking behind and a-riding before.
A stark naked drummer came walking along
With his hands in his bosom a-beating his drum.

Sat down on a hot and cold frozen stone,
Ten thousand stood round me and I was alone.
Took my heart in my hand to keep my head warm.
Ten thousand got drowned that never were born.

ANON.

A Copy of Verses on Mr Day,

WHO FROM HIS LANDLORD RAN AWAY

Here Day and Night conspired a sudden flight,
For Day, they say, has run away by Night.
Day's past and gone. Why, landlord, where's your rent?
Did you not see that Day was almost spent?
Day pawned and sold, and put off what he might;
Though it be ne'er so dark, Day will be light.
You had one Day a tenant, and would fain
Your eyes could see that Day but once again.
No, landlord, no; now you may truly say
(And to your cost, too), you have lost the Day.
Day is departed in a mist, I fear,
For Day is broke, and yet does not appear.

*

But how now, landlord, what's the matter, pray?
What! You can't sleep, you long so much for Day?
Cheer up, then, man; what though you've lost a sum,
Do you not know that pay-day yet will come?
I will engage, do you but leave your sorrow,
My life for yours, Day comes again tomorrow;
And for your rent – never torment your soul,
You'll quickly see Day peeping through a hole.

ANON.

Susan Simpson

Sudden swallows swiftly skimming,
    Sunset's slowly spreading shade,
Silvery songsters sweetly singing
    Summer's soothing serenade.

Susan Simpson strolled sedately,
    Stifling sobs, suppressing sighs.
Seeing Stephen Slocum, stately
    She stopped, showing some surprise.

'Say', said Stephen, 'sweetest sigher;
    Say, shall Stephen spouseless stay?'
Susan, seeming somewhat shyer,
    Showed submissiveness straightway.

Summer's season slowly stretches,
    Susan Simpson Slocum she —
So she signed some simple sketches —
    Soul sought soul successfully.

*

Six Septembers Susan swelters;
    Six sharp seasons snow supplies;
Susan's satin sofa shelters
    Six small Slocums side by side.

ANON.

Elegy

to the Memory of Miss Emily Kay, cousin to Miss Ellen Gee, of Kew
who died lately at Ewell, and was buried in Essex

'They fool me to the top of my bent.'—SHAKESPEARE

Sad nymphs of UL, U have much to cry for,
    Sweet MLEKU never more shall C!
O S X Maids! come hither and D, O,
    With tearful I, this MTLEG.

Without X S she did X L alway,
    Ah me! it truly vexes 1 2 C,
How soon so D R a creature may D K,
    And only leave behind X U V E!

Whate'er 10 to do she did discharge,
  So that an NME it might NDR:
Then why an SA write?—then why N
  Or with my briny tears BDU her BR?

When her Piano-40 she did press,
  Such heavenly sounds did MN8, that she
Knowing her Q, soon 1U2 confess
  Her XLNC in an XTC.

Her hair was soft as silk, not YRE,
  It gave no Q, nor yet 2P to view:
She was not handsome: shall I tell UY?
  UR2 know her I was all SQ.

L8 she was, and prattling like a J;
  How little, MLE! did you 4C,
The grave should soon MUU, cold as clay,
  And you should cease to be an NTT!

While taking T at Q with LNG,
  The MT grate she rose to put a :
Her clothes caught fire—no 1 again shall see
  Poor MLE; who now is dead as Solon.

OLNG! in vain you set at 0
  GR and reproach her for suffering 2B
Thus sacrificed; to JLU should be brought,
  Or burnt U02B in FEG.

Sweet MLEK into SX they bore,
  Taking good care the monument 2Y10,
And as her tomb was much 2 low B4,
  They lately brought fresh bricks the walls to 10
        (heighten).

                                    HORACE SMITH

Tim Turpin

Tim Turpin he was gravel-blind,
    And ne'er had seen the skies:
For Nature, when his head was made,
    Forgot to dot his eyes.

So, like a Christmas pedagogue,
    Poor Tim was forced to do –
Look out for pupils; for he had
    A vacancy for two.

There's some have specs to help their sight
    Of objects dim and small:
But Tim had *specks* within his eyes,
    And could not see at all.

Now Tim he wooed a servant maid,
    And took her to his arms;
For he, like Pyramus, had cast
    A wall-eye on her charms.

By day she led him up and down
    Where'er he wished to jog;
A happy wife, altho' she led
    The life of any dog.

But just when Tim had lived a month
    In honey with his wife,
A surgeon oped his Milton eyes,
    Like oysters with a knife.

But when his eyes were opened thus,
    He wished them dark again:
For when he looked upon his wife,
    He saw her very plain.

Her face was bad, her figure worse,
    He couldn't bear to eat:
For she was anything but like
    A Grace before his meat.

Now Tim he was a feeling man:
    For when his sight was thick,
It made him feel for everything –
    But that was with a stick.

So, with a cudgel in his hand –
    It was not light or slim –
He knock'd at his wife's head until
    It opened unto him.

And when the corpse was stiff and cold,
    He took his slaughter'd spouse,
And laid her in a heap with all
    The ashes of her house.

But, like a wicked murderer,
    He lived in constant fear
From day to day, and so he cut
    His throat from ear to ear.

The neighbours fetch'd a doctor in:
    Said he, 'This wound I dread
Can hardly be sewed up – his life
    Is hanging on a thread.'

But when another week was gone,
    He gave him stronger hope –
Instead of hanging on a thread,
    Of hanging on a rope.

Ah! when he hid his bloody work
    In ashes round about,

How little he supposed the truth
    Would soon be sifted out.

But when the parish dustman came,
    His rubbish to withdraw,
He found more dust within the heap
    Than he contracted for!

A dozen men, to try the fact,
    Were sworn that very day;
But, tho' they all were jurors, yet
    No conjurers were they.

Said Tim unto those jurymen,
    'You need not waste your breath,
For I confess myself at once
    The author of her death.

'And, oh! when I reflect upon
    The blood that I have spilt,
Just like a button is my soul,
    Inscribed with double *guilt*!'

Then turning round his head again,
    He saw before his eyes,
A great judge, and a little judge,
    The judges of a – size!

The great judge took his judgement cap
    And put it on his head,
And sentenced Tim by law to hang
    Till he was three times dead.

So he was tried, and he was hung
    (Fit punishment for such)
On Horsham drop, and none can say
    It was a drop too much.

                    THOMAS HOOD

Sonnet to Vauxhall

The cold transparent ham is on my fork —
    It hardly rains — and hark the bell! — ding-dingle —
Away. Three thousand feet at gravel work,
    Mocking a Vauxhall shower! — Married and Single
Crush — rush! — Soaked Silks with wet white Satin mingle.
    Hengler! Madame! round whom all bright sparks lurk,
Calls audibly on Mr and Mrs Pringle
    To study the Sublime, &c. — (vide Burke)
All noses are upturn'd! Whish — ish! — On high
    The rocket rushes — trails — just steals in sight —
Then droops and melts in bubbles of blue light —
    And Darkness reigns — Then balls flare up and die —
Wheels whiz — smack crackers — serpents twist — and then
    Back to the cold transparent ham again.

                        THOMAS HOOD

Evening

BY A TAILOR

Day hath put on his jacket, and around
His burning bosom buttoned it with stars.
Here will I lay me on the velvet grass,
That is like padding to earth's meagre ribs,
And hold communion with the things about me.
Ah me! how lovely is the golden braid
That binds the skirt of night's descending robe!
The thin leaves, quivering on their silken threads,
Do make a music like to rustling satin,
As the light breezes smooth their downy nap.

Ha! what is this that rises to my touch,
So like a cushion? Can it be a cabbage?
It is, it is that deeply injured flower

Which boys do flout us with; – but yet I love thee,
Thou giant rose, wrapped in a green surtout.
Doubtless in Eden thou didst blush as bright
As these, thy puny brethren; and thy breath
Sweetened the fragrance of her spicy air:
But now thou seemst like a bankrupt beau,
Stripped of his gaudy hues and essences,
And growing portly in his sober garments.

Is that a swan that rides upon the water?
O no, it is that other gentle bird,
Which is the patron of our noble calling.
I well remember, in my early years,
When these young hands first closed upon a goose;
I have a scar upon my thimble finger,
Which chronicles the hour of young ambition.
My father was a tailor, and his father,
And my sire's grandsires, all of them were tailors;
They had an ancient goose, – it was an heirloom
From some remoter tailor of our race.
It happened I did see it on a time
When none was near, and I did deal with it,
And it did burn me – oh, most fearfully!

It is a joy to straighten out one's limbs,
And leap elastic from the level counter,
Leaving the petty grievances of earth,
The breaking thread, the din of clashing shears,
And all the needles that do wound the spirit,
For such a pensive hour of soothing silence.
King Nature, shuffling in her loose undress,
Lays bare her shady bosom; – I can feel
With all around me; – I can hail the flowers
That sprig earth's mantle, – and yon quiet bird,
That rides the stream, is to me as a brother.

The vulgar know not all the hidden pockets
Where Nature stows away her loveliness.
But this unnatural posture of the legs
Cramps my extended calves, and I must go
Where I can coil them in their wonted fashion.

OLIVER WENDELL HOLMES

Jabberwocky

'Twas brillig, and the slithy toves
    Did gyre and gimble in the wabe:
All mimsy were the borogroves,
    And the mome raths outgrabe.

'Beware the Jabberwock, my son!
    The jaws that bite, the claws that catch!
Beware the Jubjub bird, and shun
    The frumious Bandersnatch!'

He took his vorpal sword in hand:
    Long time the manxome foe he sought —
So rested he by the Tumtum tree,
    And stood awhile in thought.

And, as in uffish thought he stood,
    The Jabberwock, with eyes of flame,
Came whiffling through the tulgy wood,
    And burbled as it came!

One, two! One, two! And through and through
    The vorpal blade went snicker-snack!
He left it dead, and with its head
    He went galumphing back.

'And hast thou slain the Jabberwock?
  Come to my arms, my beamish boy!
O frabjous day! Callooh! Callay!'
  He chortled in his joy.

'Twas brillig, and the slithy toves
  Did gyre and gimble in the wabe:
All mimsy were the borogroves,
  And the mome raths outgrabe.

LEWIS CARROLL

The Little Man that had a Little Gun

In stature, the Manlet was dwarfish –
  No burly big Blunderbore he:
And he wearily gazed on the crawfish
  His Wifelet had dressed for his tea.
'Now reach me, sweet Atom, my gunlet,
  And hurl the old shoelet for luck:
Let me hie to the bank of the runlet,
    And shoot thee a Duck!'

She has reached him his minikin gunlet:
  She has hurled the old shoelet for luck:
She is busily baking a bunlet,
  To welcome him home with his Duck.
On he speeds, never wasting a wordlet,
  Though thoughtlets cling, closely as wax,
To the spot where the beautiful birdlet
    So quietly quacks.

Where the Lobsterlet lurks, and the Crablet
  So slowly and sleepily crawls:
Where the Dolphin's at home, and the Dablet
  Pays long ceremonious calls:

Where the grublet is sought by the Froglet:
    Where the Frog is pursued by the Duck:
Where the Ducklet is chased by the Doglet —
        So runs the world's luck!

He has loaded with bullet and powder:
    His footfall is noiseless as air:
But the Voices grow louder and louder,
    And bellow, and bluster, and blare.
They bristle before him and after,
    They flutter above and below,
Shrill shriekings of lubberly laughter,
        Weird wailings of woe!

They echo without him, within him:
    They thrill through his whiskers and beard:
Like a teetotum seeming to spin him,
    With sneers never hitherto sneered.
'Avengement', they cry, 'on our Foelet!
    Let the Manikin weep for our wrongs!
Let us drench him, from toplet to toelet,
        With Nursery-Songs!

'He shall muse upon "Hey! Diddle! Diddle!"
    On the Cow that surmounted the Moon:
He shall rave of the Cat and the Fiddle,
    And the Dish that eloped with the Spoon:
And his soul shall be sad for the Spider,
    When Miss Muffet was sipping her whey,
That so tenderly sat down beside her,
        And scared her away!

'The music of Midsummer-madness
    Shall sting him with many a bite,
Till, in rapture of rollicking sadness,
    He shall groan with a gloomy delight:

He shall swathe him, like mists of the morning,
    In platitudes luscious and limp,
Such as deck, with a deathless adorning,
        The Song of the Shrimp!

'When the Ducklet's dark doom is decided,
    We will trundle him home in a trice:
And the banquet, so plainly provided,
    Shall round into rose-buds and rice:
In a blaze of pragmatic invention
    He shall wrestle with Fate, and shall reign:
But he has not a friend fit to mention,
        So hit him again!'

He has shot it, the delicate darling!
    And the Voices have ceased from their strife:
Not a whisper of sneering or snarling,
    As he carries it home to his wife:
Then cheerily champing the bunlet
    His spouse was so skilful to bake,
He hies him once more to the runlet,
        To fetch her the Drake!

LEWIS CARROLL

Belagcholly Days

Chilly Dovebber with his boadigg blast
    Dow cubs add strips the bedow add the lawd,
Eved October's suddy days are past —
        Add Subber's gawd!

I kdow dot what it is to which I cligg
    That stirs to sogg add sorrow, yet I trust
That still I sigg, but as the liddets sigg —
        Because I bust.

Add now, farewell to roses add to birds,
  To larded fields and tigkligg streablets eke;
Farewell to all articulated words
    I fain would speak.

Farewell, by cherished strolliggs od the sward,
  Greed glades and forest shades, farewell to you;
With sorrowing heart I, wretched add forlord,
    Bid you – achew!!!

ANON.

The Parterre

I don't know any greatest treat
As sit him in a gay parterre,
And sniff one up the perfume sweet
Of every roses buttoning there.

It only want my charming miss
Who make to blush the self red rose;
Oh! I have envy of to kiss
The end's tip of her splendid nose.

Oh! I have envy of to be
What grass 'neath her pantoffle push,
And too much happy seemeth me
The margaret which her vestige crush.

But I will meet her nose at nose,
And take occasion for her hairs,
And indicate her all my woes,
That she in fine agree my prayers.

I don't know any greatest treat
As sit him in a gay parterre,

With Madame who is too more sweet
Than every roses buttoning there.

E. H. PALMER

The Rhyme of the Rusher

IN APPROPRIATE RHYMING SLANGUAGE

I was out one night on the strict teetote,
    'Cause I couldn't afford a drain;
I was wearing a leaky I'm afloat,
    And it started to France and Spain.
But a toff was mixed in a bull and cow,
    And I helped him to do a bunk;
He had been on the I'm so tap, and now
    He was slightly elephant's trunk.

He offered to stand me a booze, so I
    Took him round to the 'Mug's Retreat';
And my round the houses I tried to dry
    By the Anna Maria's heat.
He stuck to the I'm so to drown his cares,
    While I went for the far and near,
Until the clock on the apples and pears
    Gave the office for us to clear.

Then round at the club we'd another bout,
    And I fixed him at nap until
I had turned his skyrockets inside out,
    And had managed my own to fill.
Of course I had gone on the half-ounce trick
    And we quarrelled and came to blows;
But I fired him out of the Rory quick,
    And he fell on his I suppose.

And he laid there, weighing out prayers at me,
   Without hearing the plates of meat
Of a slop, who pinched him for 'd. and d.'
   And disturbing a peaceful beat.
And I smiled as I closed my two mince pies
   In my insect promenade;
For out of his nibs I had taken a rise,
   And his stay on the spot was barred.

Next morning I brushed up my Barnet Fair,
   And got myself up pretty smart;
Then I sallied forth with a careless air,
   And contented raspberry tart.
At the first big pub I resolved, if pos.,
   That I'd sample my lucky star;
So I passed a flimsy on to the boss
   Who served drinks at the there you are.

He looked at the note, and the air began
   With his language to pen and ink
For the mug I'd fleeced had been his head man
   And had done him for lots of chink.
I'm blessed if my luck doesn't hum and ha,
   For I argued the point with skill;
But the once a week made me go ta-ta
   For a month on the can't keep still.

                    DOSS CHIDERDOSS

The Beess Song

Thousandz of thornz there be
On the Rozez where gozez
The Zebra of Zee:
Sleek, striped and hairy,
The steed of the Fairy
Princess of Zee.

Heavy with blossomz be
The Rozez that growzez
In the thickets of Zee.
Where grazez the Zebra,
Marked Abracadeebra
Of the Princess of Zee.

And he nozez the pozies
Of the Rozez that growzez
So luvez'm and free,
With an eye, dark and wary,
In search of a Fairy,
Whose Rozez he knowzez
Were not honeyed for he,
But to breathe a sweet incense
To solace the Princess
Of far-away Zee.

WALTER DE LA MARE

The Lass o' the Lab

A MODERN FOLKSONG

On being asked by an F.R.S. – no less – why modern poetry was so little inspired by Science. To the tune of *The Bailiff's Daughter of Islington*.

Now there once was a lass and a very pretty lass,
    And she was an isotope's daughter
And they called her Ethyl-Methyl, for her mother was a gas
    Made of Ch_{17} and water.

She was built on such lines, perhaps parallel lines,
    (For Einstein says they'll never meet),
And her lips resembled the most delicate sines,
    And her cheeks were like cosines sweet.

Her hair it was like transformers in a way,
    And her eyes like two live coils,
While as for her spectrum, I always used to say,
    'I could watch it till it boils'.

Though at making of love I never was a dab,
    We were soon on the best of terms,
In fact the first time that I saw her in the lab.
    We generated n^2 therms.

Her metabolisms I shall never forget
    Nor her parallaxes till I die,
But the sad thing is that, whenever we met,
    The sparks they used to fly.

Alas and alack! it was ever, ever thus;
    We had perforce to part,
For she – she was a *minus*, and I – I was a *plus*;
    In fact we were poles apart.

ENVOI

Still, Scientists all, I am sorry I was wrong,
    And $\pm$ o·3
With the Higher Hydrocarbons now shall decorate my song
    Instead of the willow-tree.

                    SIR J. C. SQUIRE

'Il est Cocu – Le Chef de Gare'

The Teuton sang the 'Wacht am Rhein'
    And 'Lieber Augustin', while we
Had 'Long Long Trail' and 'Clementine'
    And 'Old Kit-Bag' (to give but three):
    Good songs, and yet, you must agree,

The *Poilu*'s theme was richer, vaster,
    Double-distilled felicity!
'He has been duped – the station-master!'

A joyous thought, an anodyne
    For gelignite and T.N.T.;
A song to cure those saturnine
    Red singing-men of Battersea;
    And, whosoever wrote it, he
Deserves a tomb of alabaster,
    Graven on which these words should be:
'He has been duped – the station-master!'

When I am tired of Gertrude Stein
    ('She said she said that she said she ... !')
When the expressionistic line
    Has palled and Sitwells weary me,
    When bored with psycho-prosody,
Obscurist and grammaticaster,
    Give me that song of Picardy:
'He has been duped – the station-master!'

ENVOI

    Prince, did you hear the soldiery
Singing of that obscure disaster –
    (Zenith of Gallic pleasantry!)
'He has been duped – the station-master!'

                              H. S. MACKINTOSH

Ballade of Unexampled Erudition

How many people know an Asymptote?
  How many know the rules of village whist?
Or grasp the import of a *table d'hôte*
  When *Potage Président Truman* heads the list?
  I know them all: I know how ants exist,
And how to hold a golf-club or a bat:
  And how to be a prosperous dramatist —
I've got a little book which tells me that.

In a debate at Hove on 'Serb *v.* Croat',
  There up and spake Lord Bilge, economist,
But question-time arrived before the vote
  And then things took a very tiresome twist:
  When asked: 'Are *you* an Ultramontanist?'
And: 'When and why and what's a thermostat?'
  The fool was stumped and all the audience hissed.
I've got a little book which tells me that!

But knowledge is Romance's antidote:
  I know the stuff of which the stars consist,
That H_2O's prismatic drops promote
  The moonbow and the ocean's amethyst,
  And that each lover who has 'toyed and kissed'
And each whose heart has beat Love's pit-a-pat
  Tends to become a Galactophagist —
I've got a little book which tells me that.

ENVOI

Prince, when you feel my fervent foot and fist,
How nice to quote 'Bis dat qui cito dat!'
  That means . . . but there, that's something that you've missed:
I've got a little book which tells me that.

                                        H. S. MACKINTOSH

What'll Be the Title?

O to scuttle from the battle and to settle on an atoll far from brutal
    mortal neath a wattle portal!
To keep little mottled cattle and to whittle down one's chattels and
    not hurtle after brittle yellow metal!
To listen, non-committal, to the anecdotal local tittle-tattle on a
    settle round the kettle,
Never startled by a rattle more than betel-nuts a-prattle or the
    myrtle-petals' subtle throttled chortle!
But I'll bet that what'll happen if you footle round an atoll is you'll
    get in rotten fettle living totally on turtle, nettles, cuttle-fish
    or beetles, victuals fatal to the natal *élan-vital*,
And hit the bottle.
I guess I'd settle
For somewhere ethical and practical like Bootle.

JUSTIN RICHARDSON

Soldier

When the Sex War ended with the slaughter of the Grandmothers
They found a bachelor's baby suffocating under them;
Somebody called him George and that was the end of it:
    They hitched him up to the Army.
    George, you old débutante,
    How did you get in the army?

In the Retreat from Reason he deserted on his rocking-horse
And lived on a fairy's kindness till he tired of kicking her;
He smashed her spectacles and stole her cheque-book and
    mackintosh
    Then cruised his way back to the Army.

> *George, you old numero,*
> *How did you get in the Army?*

Before the Diet of Sugar he was using razor-blades
And exited soon after with an allergy to maidenheads;
He discovered a cure of his own, but no one would patent it,
> So he showed up again in the Army.
> *George, you old flybynight,*
> *How did you get in the Army?*

When the Vice Crusades were over he was hired by some Muscovites
Prospecting for deodorants among the Eskimos;
He was caught by a common cold and condemned to the whiskey mines,
> But schemozzled back to the Army.
> *George, you old Emperor,*
> *How did you get in the Army?*

Since Peace was signed with Honour he's been minding his business;
But, whoops, here comes His idleness, buttoning his uniform;
Just in tidy time to massacre the Innocents;
> He's come home to roost in the Army.
> *George, you old matador*
> *Welcome back to the Army.*

W. H. AUDEN

Calling Spring VII – MMMC

As an old traveller, I am indebted to paper-bound thrillers,
Because you travel faster from Cleveland to Terre Haute when you
travel with a lapful of victims and killers.

I am by now an authority on thumbprints and fingerprints and even
        kneeprints,
But there is one mystery I have never been able to solve in certain
        of my invaluable reprints.
I am happily agog over their funerals, which are always satisfac-
        torily followed by exhumerals,
But I can't understand why so many of them carry their copyright
        lines in Roman numerals.
I am just as learned as can be,
But if I want to find out when a book was first published, I have to
        move my lips and count on my fingers to translate Copy-
        right MCMXXXIII into Copyright 1933.
I have a horrid suspicion
That something lies behind the publisher's display of erudition.
I may be oversensitive to clues,
But I detect a desire to obfuscate and confuse.
Do they think that because a customer cannot translate
        MCMXXXIII into 1933 because he is not a classical
        scholar,
He will therefore assume the book to have been first published
        yesterday and will therefore sooner lay down his XXV
        cents or I/IV of a dollar?
Or do they, straying equally far from the straight and narrow,
Think that the scholarly will snatch it because the Roman copy-
        right line misleads him to believe it the work of Q. Horatius
        Flaccus or P. Virgilius Maro?
Because anyone can make a mistake when dealing with MCMs and
        XLVs and things, even Jupiter, ruler of gods and men;
All the time he was going around with IO he pronounced it Ten

OGDEN NASH

The Roadside Littérateur

There's a little old fellow and he has a little paintpot,
And a paucity of brushes is something that he ain't got,
And when he sees a road sign, the road sign he betters,
And expresses of himself by eliminating letters.

> Thus THROUGH ROAD
> Becomes ROUGH ROAD
> And CURVES DANGEROUS
> Is transformed to CURVES ANGER US
> And 24-HOUR SERVICE
> Turns into 24-HOUR VICE
> And MEN AT WORK IN ENTRANCE
> Is reduced to MEN AT WORK IN TRANCE
> And SLOW DOWN BRIDGE ONE WAY
> Is triumphantly condensed to
> LOW DOWN BRIDE ON WAY

But the old fellow feels a slight dissatisfaction
With the uninspiring process of pure subtraction.
The evidence would indicate he's taken as his mission
The improvement of the road signs by the process of addition.

> Thus TRAFFIC LIGHT AHEAD
> Becomes TRAFFIC SLIGHT AHEAD
> And GAS AND OIL
> Is improved to GASP AND BOIL
> And simple REST ROOMS
> Appear as QUEEREST ROOMS
> And UNDERPASS ONE WAY
> Emerges as UNDERPASS GONE AWAY
> And (perhaps his masterpiece)
>   RIGHT
>   EAST BOUND
>   TUNNEL

Is elaborated to
                    FRIGHTENED
                BEASTS ABOUND
                IN TUNNEL
Thus we see the critical mood
Becomes the creative attitude.

                                        MORRIS BISHOP

Rhyme without Reason, or Major Melhuish and the Corncrake

The bosun's mate gazed out to sea
    And his trainer's face was grey,
It looked all up with the referee,
For the meter stood at eleven-three
    And his beard was white with spray.

'Play up, my lads of the Forty-Third',
    Came a raucous voice from the cradle,
'Ride boldly under the enemy's guns.
Remember you're all of you white men's sons!'
    So they spanked him twice with a ladle.

It was dark when the visiting team got home
    With a new world's record for gliding;
We gave them tea in an aerodrome
And stuffed them with hairs from a honeycomb
    And switched them into a siding.

Rock-a-bye, rock-a-bye, close your eyes,
    It's been a record gate;
The air is thick with custard-pies
And a mule drifts by in the cloudless skies
    On a single roller-skate.

Oh, who can tell what the dawn will bring,
    My horse is so ill-bred?
He chose five stones and he took his sling,
It's a twopenny fare and the punch goes 'Ping'.
    If you hit the ground you're dead.

We woke at last from a troubled rest
    By a brook where we'd often angled;
We thought that the bull-frogs might know best,
But some were killed in the Second Test
    And the rest were privately strangled,

It's death to sleep in a dingo's bed,
    As the great CONFUCIUS teaches.
If the sun goes down in a fiery red
You must trade the halo round your head
    For a tin of ripe cling peaches.

There's a tale they tell by the cheerful hearth
    In the glittering halls of fame,
How a prince and his lady fled to Bath,
But the pumpkin burst on the bridle-path
    And the glass fell through the frame.

Tragedy, tragedy marred the days
    Of that Beach Inspector's daughter;
She wore size eight in whale-bone stays,
She was drawn round Spain by a team of greys
    And was soluble in water.

Sauce for the gander, sauce for the goose,
    With a thorny scrub between.
If they won't get tight they won't get loose.
Why try to force them? What's the use?
    My favourite colour's green.

Finish it! Finish it! Write no more;
  My dog's a pedigree Peke, Sir.
There's an inch of dust on the pantry floor,
And seven pints by the kitchen door –
  You've been away a week, Sir.

ANTHONY HALL

A Reunion in Kensington

As I was sticking hand-bills on Prince Albert's prim anatomy
A green-faced naval colonel friend came waltzing round the back of
      me,
And since I'd often flown with him, I thought it quite absurd
To let him just dance on again without a single word.

I hailed him rather noisily by tweaking my suspenderses
And asked if he remembered that I used to be a friend of his,
He said he did with ecstasy, and warmly shook my feet,
At which I offered him a half-smoked harvest-mouse to eat.

We hailed a sliding staircase which went up into the Underground.
We missed one train quite easily, but caught it as it turned around.
We lay down on the ceiling and, with quite undue contempt,
Tore up the blue advertisements for smell-less onion scent.

He said he spent his years abroad in growing sal-volatile,
He'd always stuck the seeds in wrong, since he preferred philately.
He had a daughter now, it seemed, and three dear little wives,
Who helped him making pin-cushions, and jam from unripe chives.

But as we talked the major shaved in a far-off pomposity,
Then turning a flaming eye on me, that froze me with ferocity.
'You're not the man you was,' he says, and slid under the door,
Leaving a smell of camembert and a lucky monkey's paw.

S. J. COHEN

MOCKERY AND INVECTIVE

On Philosophers

Lofty-brow-flourishers,
    Nose-in-beard-wallowers,
Bag-and-beard-nourishers,
    Dish-and-all-swallowers,
Old-cloak-investitors,
    Barefoot-look-fashioners,
Night-private-feast-takers,
    Craft-lucubrationers,
Youth-cheaters, word-catchers, vain-glory-osophers,
Such are your seekers of virtue Philosophers.

BEN JONSON(?)

To T.M. S – E

CATECHISED IN HIS EPISTLE TO MR POPE

'What makes you write at this odd rate?'
'Why, Sir, it is to intimate.'
'What makes you steal and trifle so?'
'Why, 'tis to do as others do.'
'But there's no meaning to be seen,'
'Why, that's the very thing I mean.'

ALEXANDER POPE

Should Dennis print how once you robb'd your brother,
Traduc'd your monarch and debauched your mother;
Say what revenge on Dennis can be had,
Too dull for laughter, for reply too mad?

Of one so poor you cannot take the law;
On one so old your sword you cannot draw.
Uncag'd, then, let the harmless monster rage,
Secure in dullness, madness, want and age.

ALEXANDER POPE

Abroad and at Home

As Thomas was cudgel'd one day by his wife,
He took to the street, and fled for his life:
Tom's three dearest friends came by in the squabble,
And sav'd him at once from the shrew and the rabble;
Then ventur'd to give him some sober advice;
But Tom is a person of honour so nice,
Too wise to take counsel, too proud to take warning,
That he sent to all three a challenge next morning:
Three duels he fought, thrice ventur'd his life;
Went home, and was cudgel'd again by his wife.

JONATHAN SWIFT

Against Education

Accursed the man, whom Fate ordains, in spite,
And cruel parents teach, to read and write!
What need of letters? wherefore should we spell?
Why write our names? A mark will do as well.
Much are the precious hours of youth misspent,
In climbing Learning's rugged, steep ascent;
When to the top the bold adventurer's got,
He reigns, vain monarch, o'er a barren spot;
Whilst in the vale of Ignorance below,
Folly and Vice to rank luxuriance grow;
Honours and wealth pour in on every side,
And proud Preferment rolls her golden tide.
O'er crabbed authors life's gay prime to waste.
To cramp wild genius in the chains of taste,
To bear the slavish drudgery of schools,
And tamely stoop to every pedant's rules;
For seven long years debarr'd of liberal ease,
To plod in college trammels to degrees;

Beneath the weight of solemn toys to groan,
Sleep over books, and leave mankind unknown;
To praise each senior blockhead's threadbare tale,
And laugh till freedom blush and spirits fail;
Manhood with vile submission to disgrace,
And cap the fool, whose merit is his place,
Vice-Chancellors, whose knowledge is but small,
And Chancellors, who nothing know at all.

CHARLES CHURCHILL

King George III enters Heaven

Saint Peter sat by the celestial gate,
  And nodded o'er his keys; when, lo! there came
A wondrous noise he had not heard of late –
  A rushing sound of wind, and stream, and flame;
In short, a roar of things extremely great,
  Which would have made aught save a saint exclaim;
But he, with first a start and then a wink,
  Said, 'There's another star gone out, I think!'

But ere he could return to his repose,
  A cherub flapp'd his right wing o'er his eyes –
At which St Peter yawn'd, and rubb'd his nose:
  'Saint porter', said the angel, 'prithee rise!'
Waving a goodly wing, which glow'd, as glows
  An earthly peacock's tail, with heavenly dyes:
To which the saint replied, 'Well, what's the matter?
  Is Lucifer come back with all this clatter?'

'No,' quoth the cherub: 'George the Third is dead.'
  'And who *is* George the Third?' replied the apostle:
'What George? What Third?' 'The king of England,' said
  The angel. 'Well, he won't find kings to jostle
Him on his way; but does he wear his head?
  Because the last we saw here had a tustle.

And ne'er would have got into heaven's good graces
Had he not flung his head in all our faces

'He was, if I remember, king of France;
　　That head of his, that could not keep a crown
On earth, yet ventured in my face to advance
　　A claim to those of martyrs – like my own:
If I had had my sword, as I had once
　　When I cut ears off, I had cut him down;
But having but my *keys*, and not my brand,
I only knock'd his head from out his hand.

'And then he set up such a headless howl,
　　That all the saints came out and took him in;
And there he sits by St Paul, cheek by jowl;
　　That fellow Paul – the parvenu! The skin
Of St Bartholomew, which makes his cowl
　　In heaven, and upon earth redeem'd his sin,
So as to make a martyr, never sped
Better than did this weak and wooden head.

But had it come up here upon its shoulders,
　　There would have been a different tale to tell:
The fellow-feeling in the saint's beholders
　　Seems to have acted on them like a spell,
And so this very foolish head heaven solders
　　Back on its trunk: it may be very well,
And seems the custom here to overthrow
Whatever has been wisely done below.'

The angel answer'd, 'Peter! do not pout:
　　The king who comes has head and all entire,
And never knew much what it was about –
　　He did as doth the puppet – by its wire,
And will be judged like all the rest, no doubt:
　　My business and your own is not to inquire

Into such matters, but to mind our cue –
Which is to act as we are bid to do.'

GEORGE GORDON, LORD BYRON

Rhymes on the Road

And is there then no earthly place
    Where we can rest, in dream Elysian,
Without some curst, round English face
    Popping up near, to break the vision?
'Mid northern lakes and southern vines,
    Unholy cits we're doomed to meet;
Nor highest Alps nor Appenines
    Are sacred from Threadneedle Street!

If up the Simplon's path we wind,
Fancying we leave this world behind,
Such pleasant sounds salute one's ear
As – 'Baddish news from 'Change, my dear –
The Funds – (phew, curse this ugly hill) –
Are low'ring fast – (what, higher still?)
And – (zooks, we're mounting up to heaven!) –
Will soon be down to sixty-seven.'

Go where we may – rest where we will,
Eternal London haunts us still.
The trash of Almack's or Fleet Ditch –
And scarce a pin's head difference *which* –
Mixes, though ev'n to Greece, we run,
With every rill from Helicon!
And, if this rage for travelling lasts,
If Cockneys, of all sects and castes,
Old maidens, aldermen, and squires,
Will leave their puddings and coal fires,
To gape at things in foreign lands,
No soul among them understands;

If Blues desert their coteries,
  To show off 'mong the Wahabees;
If neither sex nor age controls,
    Nor fear of Mamelukes forbids
Young ladies, with pink parasols,
    To glide among the Pyramids –
Why, then, farewell all hope to find
A spot that's free from London-kind!
Who knows, if to the West we roam,
But we may find some *Blue* 'at home'
    Among the *Blacks* of Carolina –
Or, flying to the Eastward, see
    Some Mrs HOPKINS taking tea
        And toast upon the Wall of China!

                              THOMAS MOORE

Cologne

In Köln, a town of monks and bones,
And pavements fang'd with murderous stones
And rags, and hags, and hideous wenches;
I counted two and seventy stenches,
All well defined, and several stinks!
Ye Nymphs that reign o'er sewers and sinks,
The river Rhine, it is well known,
Doth wash your city of Cologne;
But tell me, Nymphs, what power divine
Shall henceforth wash the river Rhine?

                              S. T. COLERIDGE

Swans sing before they die – 'twere no bad thing
Should certain persons die before they sing.

                              S. T. COLERIDGE

Fame

Fame, like other tawdry wares,
At best will last a thousand years
But often somewhat earlier
Shows signs of fading, wear and tear.

A butterfly most dandified,
As Swallowtail known far and wide,
The finest knight his age could muster,
Now here, now there would greet each cluster
Of blossoms and with 'Oh' and 'Ah'
Sip nectar and ambrosia.

When of this feasting he grew tired
He'd rest outspread, while all admired
The splendour of his decorations;
Rightly, his fame reached all the nations.

Young girls, on seeing him, would say
That he was charming and *so* gay.

In vain the schoolboys threw their caps
To catch him. He escaped those traps.

Even the sparrow did his best,
But missed. The knight was not impressed.

But now a student who had planned
The hunt in detail tried his hand.

Soon in a net most closely wrought
The wretched fugitive he caught –
A specimen so flawless, he
Must pin it down immediately.

Thus did the knight receive a frame
Complete with label, date and name,
To rest there famous, unforgotten,
Until moth-eaten, or just rotten.

It breaks my heart, but I'm unable
To add a sequel to this fable.

WILHELM BUSCH
(translated by MICHAEL HAMBURGER)

Malines

(MIDNIGHT, JULY 4TH, 1882)

Belgian, with cumbrous tread and iron boots,
Who in the murky middle of the night
Designing to renew the foul pursuits
In which thy life is passed, ill-favoured wight,
And wishing on the platform to alight
Where thou couldst mingle with thy fellow-brutes,
Didst walk the carriage floor (a leprous sight)
As o'er the sky some baleful meteor shoots:
Upon my slippered foot thou didst descend,
Didst rouse me from my slumbers mad with pain,
And laughedst aloud for several minutes' space.
Oh mayst thou suffer tortures without end:
May fiends with glowing pincers rend thy brain,
And beetles batten on thy blackened face.

J. K. STEPHEN

On a Rhine Steamer

Republic of the West,
　　Enlightened, free, sublime,
Unquestionably best
　　Production of our time.

The telephone is thine,
　　And thine the Pullman Car,
The caucus, the divine
　　Intense electric star.

To thee we likewise owe
　　The venerable names
Of Edgar Allen Poe,
　　And Mr Henry James.

In short it's due to thee,
  Thou kind of Western star,
That we have come to be
  Precisely what we are.

But every now and then,
  It cannot be denied,
You breed a kind of men
  Who are not dignified,

Or courteous or refined,
  Benevolent or wise,
Or gifted with a mind
  Beyond the common size,

Or notable for tact,
  Agreeable to me,
Or anything, in fact,
  That people ought to be.

                    J. K. STEPHEN

Lines from a Parish Magazine

I am a loyal Anglican,
  A Rural Dean and Rector;
I keep a wife and pony-trap,
  I wear a chest-protector.
I should not like my name to be
  Connected with a party;
But still my type of service is
  Extremely bright and hearty.

Of course, one has to keep abreast
  Of changing times and manners;
A Harvest Festival we keep,
  With Special Psalms and banners;

A Flower-Service in July,
    A Toy-Fund Intercession,
And, when the hens lay well, we hope
    To start an Egg-Procession.

My wife and I composed a form
    For dedicating hassocks,
Which (slightly changed) we also use
    For surplices and cassocks;
Our Bishop, when we sent it for
    His Lordship's approbation,
Remarked: 'A very primitive
    And pleasing compilation.'

To pick the best from every school
    The object of my art is,
And steer a middle course between
    The two contending parties.
My own opinions would no doubt
    Be labelled 'High' by many;
But all know well I could not wish
    To give offence to any.

One ought, I'm certain, to produce
    By gradual education
A tone of deeper Churchmanship
    Throughout the population.
There are, I doubt not, even here
    Things to be done in plenty;
But still – you know the ancient saw –
    'Festina lentè – *lentè*.'

I humbly feel that my success,
    My power of attraction,
Is mainly due to following
    This golden rule of action:

'See us from all men's point of view,
    Use all men's eyes to see with,
And never preach what anyone
    Could ever disagree with.'

G. W. E. RUSSELL

To Julia, in Envy of her Toughness

When I, in such revolting weather
    As permeates the Arctic zone,
Just keep my soul and flesh together
    By wearing things that weigh a stone,
And find that you go undefeated
    In clothes that let the blast blow through,
I marvel why my sex is treated
    As much the tougher of the two.

When Earth is wrapt in frosty vapour
    And barren boughs with snow are fledged,
Your callous legs still love to caper
    In summer hose of silk (alleged);
While I, if thus I mocked the blizzard
    Or rashly dared the bitter rime –
I should be stricken in the gizzard,
    I should be dead in three days' time.

Having survived the day's exposure
    At eve you bare your hardy spine,
Marking that exhibition's closure
    At well below the old waist-line;
This seems to cause your lungs no trouble,
    Yet if I danced *sans* shirt and vest
I should incur pneumonia (double)
    And in a week or so go West.

How comes it you enjoy a measure
    Of nudity to me denied?
Is it because your frame, my treasure,
    Is coated with a coarser hide?
I fear you'll deem this view abhorrent,
    So let me add, to break, the blow
You are – and will remain, I warrant –
    The nicest pachyderm I know.

SIR OWEN SEAMAN

By Deputy

As Shakespeare couldn't write his plays
    (If Mrs Gallup's not mistaken)
I think how wise in many ways
    He was to have them done by Bacon;
They might have mouldered on the shelf,
    Mere minor dramas (and he knew it!)
If he had written them himself
    Instead of letting Bacon do it.

And if it's true, as Brown and Smith
    In many learned tomes have stated,
That Homer was an idle myth
    He ought to be congratulated,
Since thus, evading birth, he rose
    For men to worship at a distance:
He might have penned inferior prose
    Had he achieved a real existence.

To him and Shakespeare men agree
    In making very nice allusions;
But no one thinks of praising me,
    For I compose my own effusions:

As others wrote *their* works divine
   And they immortal thus today are,
Perhaps had some one written mine
   I might have been as great as they are.

A. ST JOHN ADCOCK

Satire on Paying Calls in August

When I was young, throughout the hot season
There were no carriages driving about the roads.
People shut their doors and lay down in the cool:
Or if they went out, it was not to pay calls.
Nowadays – ill-bred, ignorant fellows,
When they feel the heat, make for a friend's house.
The unfortunate host, when he hears someone coming
Scowls and frowns, but can think of no escape.
'There's nothing for it but to rise and go to the door,'
And in his comfortable seat he groans and sighs.

*

The conversation does not end quickly:
Prattling and babbling, what a lot he says!
Only when one is almost dead with fatigue
He asks at last if one isn't finding him tiring.
(One's arm is almost in half with continual fanning:
The sweat is pouring down one's neck in streams.)
Do not say that this is a small matter:
I consider the practice a blot on our social life.
I therefore caution all wise men
That August visitors should not be admitted.

CH'ĒNG HSIAO
(translated by ARTHUR WALEY)

Paean

Friends of the Rich! whom danger never daunts,
Who tend the Wealthy in their frightful haunts,
Sharing the anguish of their mournful days,
Steadfast to help, to comfort, cheer and praise —
Stout souls, work on! A silver soup-tureen
Once more has caught Miss Busy on the bean;
Propelled by menial feet through Berkeley Square,
Poor Mrs Pegaway has got the air;
In Green Street Mr Freddie's lost his pants;
'Auntie's' been murdered by the rich in Hants,
And Percy, victim of a wild carouse,
Has just been thrown off two more yachts at Cowes;
Miss Upcher's better, though not free from pain,
But Archie Gowle, alas, will never walk again. ...
They humbly strove; their task was long and grim,
Oft were they playthings of a moneyed whim,
Now welcomed, now expelled with angry shrieks,
Plied with champagne, or gnawed by wayward Pekes:
Be this their guerdon in a glorious cause —
They loved the Rich, whom all the world abhors.

D. B. WYNDHAM LEWIS

On the Prevalence of Literary Revivals

It's hard
Keeping up with the *avant-garde*.
There was the time when Donne
Had a place in the sun.
His *lettres* were *belles* of pure gold
And they tolled and they tolled and they tolled,
Until critics in suitable haunts
Took up Kafka (Franz).

Then everyone wanted to herald
The genius of Scott Fitzgerald.
After that, among Prominent Names,
It was utterly Henry James.

In between, of course, there was room
For a Melville boom,
For a peek at Poe, for a dollop
Of Trollope,
And currently people report on
A scrambling aboard
The elegant wagons of Wharton
and Ford Madox Ford.

Oh, it's perfectly clear
That there's change when the critics forgather.
Last year was a Hawthorne year.
Coming up – Willa Cather?
And I'm happy the great ones are thriving,
But what puzzles my head
Is the thought that they needed reviving.
I had never been told they were dead.

PHYLLIS MCGINLEY

The Playboy of the Demi-World: 1938

Aloft in Heavenly Mansions, Doubleyou One –
Just Mayfair flats, but certainly sublime –
You'll find the abode of D'Arcy Honeybunn,
A rose-red cissy half as old as time.

Peace cannot age him, and no war could kill
The genial tenant of those cosy rooms,
He's lived there always and he lives there still,
Perennial pansy, hardiest of blooms.

There you'll encounter aunts of either sex,
Their jokes equivocal or over-ripe,
Ambiguous couples wearing slacks and specs
And the stout Lesbian knocking out her pipe.

The rooms are crammed with flowers and *objets d'art*,
A Ganymede still hands the drinks – and plenty!
D'Arcy still keeps a rakish-looking car
And still behaves the way he did at twenty.

A ruby pin is fastened in his tie,
The scent he uses is *Adieu Sagesse*.
His shoes are suede, and as the years go by
His tailor's bill's not getting any less.

He cannot whistle, always rises late,
Is good at indoor sports and parlour-tricks,
Mauve is his favourite colour, and his gait
Suggests a pea-hen walking on hot bricks.

He prances forward with his hands outspread
And folds all comers in a gay embrace,
A wavy toupee on his hairless head,
A fixed smile on his often-lifted face.

'My dears!' he lisps, to whom all men are dear,
'How perfectly enchanting of you!' turns
Towards his guests and twitters, 'Look who's here!
Do come and help us fiddle while Rome burns!'

'The kindest man alive', so people say,
'Perpetual youth!' 'But have you seen his eyes?
The eyes of some old saurian in decay
That asks no questions and is told no lies.

Under the fribble lurks a worn-out sage
Heavy with disillusion, and alone;
So never say to D'Arcy, 'Be your age!' —
He'd shrivel up at once or turn to stone.

WILLIAM PLOMER

On a Female Snob, Surprised

Now, when you cut me dead and say that I'm
Not kennel-bred, nor pure of pedigree,
I'll think how often that old Mongrel, Time,
Has cocked a leg against your Family Tree.

PATRIC DICKINSON

Dumb Friends' Corner

She was a Phantom of Delight
When first she gleamed upon my sight;
Now for her portrait I can't fancy a
Better all-round man than Landseer.

D. B. WYNDHAM LEWIS

Call

(INCIDENT AT WEEK-END PARTY)

He cried: 'Let England to herself be true!
    What sacrifice too great if England live?
What boots it that our treasure, poured anew,
Make of us paupers, if we gladly give?'

His face was honest, and sincere, and red:
He did a bit in armaments, he said.

D. B. WYNDHAM LEWIS

STUDIED IRREVERENCE

∽

The Printers' Cauldron

Scene – A dark Room: in the middle a great cauldron burning.
Thunder – Enter three Printers' Devils.

FIRST DEVIL

Thrice the watchman gave his knock,

SECOND DEVIL

Twice, – and once has crowed the cock;

THIRD DEVIL

Our master comes, ''Tis five o'clock'.

ALL

Now your several schemes display
To make the paper of the day: –

SECOND DEVIL

Spy that standing on cold stone,
Names and titles one by one,
Catchest at the doors of fashion,
Haste to bring your motley trash in;
Packwood's puffs, and state of weather,
Hints of who and who's together,
(Paid to contradict tomorrow.
Lie – inserted to our sorrow)
Fluttering follies light as vapour,
Rise to the top o' the paper.

ALL

Double, double, toil and trouble,
Touch the cash – the nation bubble.

FIRST DEVIL

Braham – Soldier tir'd – Mad Bess –
Case of singular distress,
Speed of egotistic pleader,

String of coaches made by Leader,
Fashionable invalids,
Morning dresses, widows' weeds,
Lobby quarrels, satisfaction,
Rout in Mayfair, crim. con. action.
Patent soles that never falter,
Doctors Brodum and Sir Walter,
Pun, and *vive la bagatelle*,
Schemes to make our paper sell.

ALL AS BEFORE

THIRD DEVIL

Bonaparté, Paris fashions,
Chapels, Cyprian assignations,
Captain Sash, the sea-side shark –
Slander's arrow shot i' the dark,
Villa of Roehampton Jew,
Horrid murder done at Kew;
Queries, critical corrections,
Galvinistic resurrections,
Treatise on the moon's eclipse,
Paint for cheeks and salve for lips;
Stupid pun, birth-strangled jest –
Portsmouth letter – wind north-west. }
And thus our merit stands confest.

ALL AS BEFORE

SECOND DEVIL

Cool it with an empty boast,
That every day we sell the most. }
'Tis done – behold *The Morning Post!*

JAMES SMITH

Hiawatha's Photographing

From his shoulder Hiawatha
Took the camera of rosewood,
Made of sliding, folding rosewood;
Neatly put it all together.
In its case it lay compactly,
Folded into nearly nothing;
But he opened out the hinges,
Pushed and pulled the joints and hinges,
Till it looked all squares and oblongs,
Like a complicated figure
In the Second Book of Euclid.

   This he perched upon a tripod –
Crouched beneath its dusky cover –
Stretched his hand, enforcing silence –
Said, 'Be motionless, I beg you!'
Mystic, awful was the process.

   All the family in order
Sat before him for their pictures:
Each in turn, as he was taken,
Volunteered his own suggestions,
His ingenious suggestions.

   First the Governor, the Father:
He suggested velvet curtains
Looped about a massy pillar;
And the corner of a table,
Of a rosewood dining table.
He would hold a scroll of something.
Hold it firmly in his left-hand;
He would keep his right-hand buried
(Like Napoleon) in his waistcoat;
He would contemplate the distance
With a look of pensive meaning,

As of ducks that die in tempests.
    Grand, heroic was the notion:
Yet the picture failed entirely:
Failed, because he moved a little,
Moved, because he could not help it.
    Next his better half took courage;
She would have her picture taken.
She came dressed beyond description,
Dressed in jewels and in satin
Far too gorgeous for an empress.
Gracefully she sat down sideways,
With a simper scarcely human,
Holding in her hand a bouquet
Rather larger than a cabbage.
All the while that she was sitting,
Still the lady chattered, chattered,
Like a monkey in the forest.
'Am I sitting still?' she asked him.
'Is my face enough in profile?
Shall I hold the nosegay higher?
Will it come into the picture?'
And the picture failed completely.
    Next the son, the Stunning-Cantab:
He suggested curves of beauty,
Curves pervading all his figure,
Which the eye might follow onward,
Till they centred in the breast-pin,
Centred in the golden breast-pin.
He had learnt it all from Ruskin
(Author of 'The Stones of Venice',
'Seven Lamps of Architecture',
'Modern Painters' and some others);
And perhaps he had not fully
Understood his author's meaning;
But, whatever was the reason,
All was fruitless, as the picture

Ended in an utter failure.

Next to him the eldest daughter:
She suggested very little,
Only asked if he would take her
With her look of 'passive beauty'.

Her idea of passive beauty
Was a squinting of the left-eye,
Was a drooping of the right-eye,
Was a smile that went up sideways
To the corner of the nostrils.

Hiawatha, when she asked him,
Took no notice of the question,
Looked as if he hadn't heard it;
But, when pointedly appealed to,
Smiled in his peculiar manner,
Coughed and said it 'didn't matter',
Bit his lip and changed the subject.

Nor in this was he mistaken,
As the picture failed completely.

So in turn the other sisters.

Last the youngest son was taken:
Very rough and thick his hair was,
Very round and red his face was,
Very dusty was his jacket,
Very fidgety his manner.
And his overbearing sisters
Called him names he disapproved of:
Called him Johnny, 'Daddy's Darling',
Called him Jacky, 'Scrubby School-boy'.
And, so awful was the picture,
In comparison the others
Seemed, to one's bewildered fancy,
To have partially succeeded.

Finally my Hiawatha
Tumbled all the tribe together,
('Grouped' is not the right expression),

And, as happy chance would have it,
Did at last obtain a picture
Where the faces all succeeded:
Each came out a perfect likeness.

    Then they joined and all abused it,
Unrestrainedly abused it,
As the worst and ugliest picture
They could possibly have dreamed of.
'Giving one such strange expressions –
Sullen, stupid, pert expressions.
Really anyone would take us
(Anyone that did not know us)
For the most unpleasant people!'
(Hiawatha seemed to think so,
Seemed to think it not unlikely).
All together rang their voices,
Angry, loud, discordant voices,
As of dogs that howl in concert,
As of cats that wail in chorus.

    But my Hiawatha's patience,
His politeness and his patience,
Unaccountably had vanished,
And he left that happy party.
Neither did he leave them slowly,
With the calm deliberation,
The intense deliberation
Of a photographic artist:
But he left them in a hurry,
Left them in a mighty hurry,
Stating that he would not stand it,
Stating in emphatic language
What he'd be before he'd stand it.
Hurriedly he packed his boxes:
Hurriedly the porter trundled
On a barrow all his boxes:
Hurriedly he took his ticket:

Hurriedly the train received him:
Thus departed Hiawatha.

LEWIS CARROLL

An Allegory

WRITTEN IN DEEP DEJECTION

Once in the gardens of delight,
  I pluck'd the fairest, fullest rose;
But (while I prest its petals tight
  Against the threshold of my nose)
That loathsome centipede, Remorse,
  Invaded with a stealthy tread
My nasal organ, and of course
  Soon reached the middle of my head.

The hideous tenant crawls and creeps
  About the chambers of my brain,
He never pauses – never sleeps –
  Nor thinks of coming out again.
The movements of his hundred feet
  Are gentler than the autumn breeze;
But I dislike to feel him eat
  My cerebellum by degrees.

With snuff, tobacco, Preston salts,
  And various other potent smells,
I strive to fumigate the vaults
  In which the devastator dwells.
I pull my hair out by the root –
  I dash my head against the door –
It only makes the hateful brute
  A trifle noisier than before.

Then tell me not that Joy's bright flow'r
  Upon this canker'd heart may bloom,

Like toadstools on a time-worn tow'r,
    Or dandelions on a tomb.
I mourn departed Hope in vain,
    For briny tears may nought avail;
You cannot catch *that* bird again
    By dropping salt upon its tail!

H. S. LEIGH

Merry May

(1855)

The sky scowls,
    The wind howls,
The leaves shrivel up in folds;
    The flocks and herds
    And little birds
Are all suffering from colds:
    And my nose
    Is quite froze!
With teeth chattering away,
    Let us sing
    Severe Spring,
O miserable May!

PERCIVAL LEIGH

A Catch

BY A MIMIC OF MODERN MELODY

If you were queen of bloaters
    And I were king of soles,
The sea we'd wag our fins in,
Nor heed the crooked pins in,
The water, dropped by boaters
    To catch our heedless joles;
If you were queen of bloaters
    And I were king of soles.

If you were Lady Mile-End
    And I were Duke of Bow,
We'd marry and we'd quarrel,
And then, to point the moral,
Should Lord Penzance his file lend,
    Our chains to overthrow;
If you were Lady Mile-End
    And I were Duke of Bow.

If you were chill November
    And I were sunny June;
I'd not with love pursue you;
For I should be to woo you
(You're foggy, pray remember)
    A most egregious spoon;
If you were chill November
    And I were sunny June.

If you were cook to Venus
    And I were J. 19;
When missus was out dining,
Our suppertites combining,
We'd oft contrive between us
    To keep the platter clean;
If you were cook to Venus
    And I were J. 19.

If you were but a jingle
    And I were but a rhyme;
We'd keep this up for ever,
Nor think it very clever

A grain of sense to mingle
    At times with simple chime;
If you were but a jingle
    And I were but a rhyme.

THOMAS HOOD, junr

Poets and Linnets

Where'er there's a thistle to feed a linnet
And linnets are plenty, thistles rife –
Or an acorn cup to catch dew-drops in it,
There's ample promise of further life.
Now, mark how we begin it.

Now linnets will follow, if linnets are minded,
As blows the white feather parachute;
And ships will reel by the tempest blinded –
By ships, and shiploads of men to boot!
How deep whole fleets you'll find hid.

And we'll blow the thistle-down hither and thither,
Forgetful of linnets and men, and God.
The dew! for its want an oak will wither –
By the dull hoof into the dust is trod,
And then who strikes the cithar?

But thistles were only for donkeys intended,
And that donkeys are common enough is clear.
And that drop! what a vessel it might have befriended,
Does it add any flavour to Glugabib's beer?
Well, there's my musing ended.

THOMAS HOOD, junr

A Sonnet

Two voices are there: one is of the deep;
It learns the storm-cloud's thunderous melody,
Now roars, now murmurs with the changing sea,
Now bird-like pipes, now closes soft in sleep;
And one is of an old half-witted sheep
Which bleats articulate monotony,
And indicates that two and one are three,
That grass is green, lakes damp, and mountains steep:
And, Wordsworth, both are thine: at certain times
Forth from the heart of thy melodious rhymes
The form and pressure of high thoughts will burst:
At other times – good Lord! I'd rather be
Quite unacquainted with the ABC
Than write such hopeless rubbish as thy worst.

J. K. STEPHEN

Culture in the Slums

Now ain't they utterly too-too
    (She ses, my missus mine, ses she),
Them flymy little bits of Blue?

Joe, just you kool 'em – nice and skew
    Upon our old meogginee,
Now ain't they utterly too-too?

They're better than a pot'n a screw,
    They're equal to a Sunday spree,
Them flymy little bits of Blue!

Suppose I put 'em up the flue,
    And booze the profits, Joe? Not me.
Now ain't they utterly too-too?

I do the 'Igh Art fake, I do.
　　Joe, I'm consummate; and I see
Them flymy little bits of Blue.

Which, Joe, is why I ses to you —
　　Aesthetic-like, and limp, and free —
Now ain't they utterly too-too,
Them flymy little bits o' Blue?

W. E. HENLEY

Inspect Us

Out of the clothes that cover me
　　Tight as the skin is on the grape,
I thank whatever gods may be
　　For my unconquerable shape.

In the full clutch of bone and steel
　　I have not whined nor cried aloud;
Whatever else I may conceal,
　　I show my thoughts unshamed and proud.

The forms of other actorines
　　I put away into the shade;
All of them flossy near-blondines
　　Find and shall find me unafraid.

It matters not how straight the tape,
　　How cold the weather is, or warm —
I am the mistress of my shape —
　　I am the captain of my form.

EDITH DANIELL

A Melton Mowbray Pork-Pie

Strange pie that is almost a passion,
  O passion immoral for pie!
Unknown are the ways that they fashion,
  Unknown and unseen of the eye.
The pie that is marbled and mottled,
  The pie that digests with a sigh:
For all is not Bass that is bottled,
  And all is not pork that is pie.

                    RICHARD LE GALLIENNE

How Often

They stood on the bridge at midnight,
  In a park not far from the town;
They stood on the bridge at midnight,
  Because they didn't sit down.

The moon rose o'er the city,
  Behind the dark church spire;
The moon rose o'er the city
  And kept on rising higher.

How often, oh, how often!
  They whispered words so soft;
How often, oh, how often;
  How often, oh, how oft!

                    BEN KING

Ballad

BY HANS BREITMANN

Der noble Ritter Hugo
  Von Schwillensaufenstein,
Rode out mit shpeer and helmet,
  Und he coom to de panks of de Rhine.

Und oop der rose a meermaid,
  Vot hadn't got nodings on,
Und she say, 'Oh, Ritter Hugo,
  Vhere you goes mit yourself alone?'

And he says, 'I rides in de creenwood,
  Mit helmet und mit shpeer,
Till I cooms into em Gasthaus,
  Und dere I trinks some beer.'

Und den outshpoke de maiden
  Vot hadn't got nodings on:
'I don't dink mooch of beoplesh
  Dat goes mit demselfs alone.

'You'd petter coom down in de wasser,
  Vhere dere's heaps of dings to see,
Und hafe a shplendid tinner
  Und drafel along mit me.

'Dere you sees de fisch a schwimmin',
  Und you catches dem efery von': –
So sang dis wasser maiden
  Vot hadn't got nodings on.

'Dere ish drunks all full mit money
  In ships dat vent down ot old;

Und you helpsh yourself, by dunder!
  To shimmerin' crowns of gold.

'Shoost look at dese shpoons und vatches!
  Shoost see dese diamant rings!
Coom down and fill your bockets,
  Und I'll giss you like efery dings.

'Vot you vantsh mit your schnapps und lager?
  Coom down into der Rhine!
Der ish pottles der Kaiser Charlemagne
  Vonce filled mit gold-red wine!'

Dat fetched him – he shtood all shpell pound;
  She pooled his coat-tails down,
She drawed him oonder der wasser,
  De maiden mit nodings on.

C. G. LELAND

The Poets in the Nursery

OMAR KHAYYAM

A Sixpence and a Pocketful of Rye.
So sing I, and must sing until I die,
    And not the Garnered Wisdom of the years
Nor all the Wheeling Stars can tell me why.

Ye know the time-worn tale – a score or so
Of Blackbirds, piping plaintively below
    The Brooding horror of a monstrous Crust,
Close-huddled in a Wilderness of dough.

Yet soon the darkness lightens. For the king
Cuts deeply, and the birds are on the wing,
    The mellow-throated warblers of the woods
Burst from their flaky Prison House to sing.

I sometimes count this marvel not the least
Of all the magic splendours of the East;
    I sometimes think there never was prepared
A daintier dish to grace a Monarch's feast.

List to the solemn burden of my cry,
Ah, what it means I know not, no, not I,
    Unknown, unknowable, it haunts me still,
A Sixpence and a Pocketful of Rye.

G. F. FORREST

TENNYSON

So ever in the corner bode Sir Jack.
Called Horner, for the weird rhyme hath it so.
But so it chanced that, when the bells rang out
Their Christmas welcome through the frosty sky,
Sir Jack, still crouching in his lair, beheld
A seasonable pie, and snatched, and fain
Would eat. But first he communed with his soul
How he might work some deed of worthy note.
Then with a sudden high resolve he plunged
His thumb therein, and caught, and brought to light
A mighty plum. And o'er his visage spread
A light of large contentment, and he smiled,
Taking therefrom some credit to himself
For some mysterious reason. Then he cried:
'Henceforth let no man doubt that I am good.'

G. F. FORREST

RUDYARD KIPLING

O this I ha' heard, and this I ha' read in a book o' nursery lore,
And I make no doubt ye ha' found it out and read it all before.
But I care not, I; to the shivering sky I will bellow the tale anew,
How the shameless sheep o' the fair Bo-Peep had vanished and left
    no clue.

In a flood of tears, through the clanging spheres, to the Nethermost
    Gloom she hied,
Till she caught in despair at a comet's hair, and took up her tale and
    cried:
'O I ha' been east, and I ha' been west, I ha' waked wi' a fiendish
    yell
The Shapes that fit i' the seething Pit, I ha' sat on the rim o' Hell.
I ha' stopped to ask o' the souls that bask i' the sheen o' the Milky
    Way,
But for all my gain comes the grim refrain, "No Sheep have passed
    this way".'
From the fluttering silence stole a voice, the voice o' the Tortured
    Star,
(Ye may see his glare, if ye enter there, where the Naughty Devils
    are);
'Get hence, get hence, till ye win more sense than to climb to the
    Stars to weep.
And to vex my soul at the midmost pole for the sake o' your
    shiftless sheep.
Let be, let be. They shall yet win free and, if promise o' mine avails,
Ye shall find ('tis strange) no radical change i' the site o' their
    several tails.'

G. F. FORREST

If Gray had had to write his Elegy in the Cemetery of Spoon River instead of in that of Stoke Poges

The curfew tolls the knell of parting day,
    The whippoorwill salutes the rising moon,
And wanly glimmer in her gentle ray
    The sinuous windings of the turbid Spoon.

Here where the flattering and mendacious swarm
    Of lying epitaphs their secrets keep,
At last incapable of further harm,
    The lewd forefathers of the village sleep.

The earliest drug of half-awakened morn,
  Cocaine or hashish, strychnine, poppy-seeds
Or fiery produce of fermented corn
  No more shall start them on the day's misdeeds.

For them no more the whetstone's cheerful noise,
  No more the sun upon his daily course
Shall watch them savouring the genial joys
  Of murder, bigamy, arson and divorce.

Here they all lie; and, as the hour is late,
  O stranger, o'er their tombstones cease to stoop,
But bow thine ear to me and contemplate
  The unexpurgated annals of the group.

Here are two hundred only: yet of these
  Some thirty died of drowning in the river,
Sixteen went mad, ten others had D.T.'s,
  And twenty-eight cirrhosis of the liver.

Several by absent-minded friends were shot,
  Still more blew out their own exhausted brains,
One died of a mysterious inward rot,
  Three fell off roofs, and five were hit by trains.

One was harpooned, one gored by a bull-moose,
  Four on the Fourth fell victims to lock-jaw,
Ten in electric chair or hempen noose
  Suffered the last exaction of the law.

Stranger, you quail, and seem inclined to run;
  But, timid stranger, do not be unnerved;
I can assure you that there was not one
  Who got a tithe of what he had deserved.

Full many a vice is born to thrive unseen,
  Full many a crime the world does not discuss,

Full many a pervert lives to reach a green
　　Replete old age, and so it was with us.

Here lies a parson who would often make
　　Clandestine rendezvous with Claflin's Moll,
And 'neath the druggist's counter creep to take
　　A sip of surreptitious alcohol.

And here a doctor, who had seven wives,
　　And, fearing this *ménage* might seem grotesque,
Persuaded six of them to spend their lives
　　Locked in a drawer of his private desk.

And others here there sleep who, given scope,
　　Had writ their names large on the Scrolls of Crime,
Men who, with half a chance, might haply cope
　　With the first miscreants of recorded time.

Doubtless in this neglected spot was laid
　　Some village Nero who had missed his due,
Some Bluebeard who dissected many a maid,
　　And all for naught, since no one ever knew.

Some poor bucolic Borgia here may rest
　　Whose poisons sent whole families to their doom.
Some hayseed Herod who, within his breast,
　　Concealed the sites of many an infant's tomb.

Types that the Muse of Masefield might have stirred,
　　Or waked to ecstasy Gaboriau,
Each in his narrow cell at last interred,
　　All, all are sleeping peacefully below.

*

Enough, enough! But, stranger, ere we part,
　　Glancing farewell to each nefarious bier,

This warning I would beg you to take to heart,
  'There is an end to even the worst career!'

SIR J. C. SQUIRE

The Everlasting Percy
or Mr Masefield on the Railway Centenary

I used to be a fearful lad,
The things I did were downright bad;
And worst of all were what I done
From seventeen to twenty-one
On all the railways far and wide
From sinfulness and shameful pride.

For several years I was so wicked
I used to go without a ticket,
And travelled underneath the seat
Down in the dust of people's feet,
Or else I sat as bold as brass
And told them 'Season' in first class.
In 1921, at Harwich,
I smoked in a non-smoking carriage;
I never knew what Life nor Art meant,
I wrote 'Reserved' on my compartment,
And once (I was a guilty man)
I swapped the labels in guard's van.
From 1922 to 4
I leant against the carriage door
Without a-looking at the latch;
And once, a-leaving Colney Hatch,
I put a huge and heavy parcel
Which I were taking to Newcastle,
Entirely filled with lumps of lead,
Up on the rack above my head;
And when it tumbled down, oh Lord!

I pulled communication cord.
The guard came round and said, 'You mule!
What have you done, you dirty fool?'
I simply sat and smiled, and said
'Is this train right for Holyhead?'
He said 'You blinking blasted swine,
You'll have to pay the five-pound fine.'
I gave a false name and address,
Puffed up with my vaingloriousness.
At Bickershaw and Strood and Staines
I've often got on moving trains,
And once alit at Norwood West
Before my coach had come to rest.
A window and a lamp I broke
At Chipping Sodbury and Stoke
And worse I did at Wissendine:
I threw out bottles on the line
And other articles as be
Likely to cause great injury
To persons working on the line –
That's what I did at Wissendine.
I grew so careless what I'd do
Throwing things out, and dangerous too,
That, last and worst of all I'd done,
I threw a great sultana bun
Out of the train at Pontypridd –

*

It hit a platelayer, it did.
I thought that I should have to swing
And never hear the sweet birds sing.
The jury recommended mercy,
And that's how grace was given to Percy.

And now I have a motor-bike
And up and down the road I hike,

Seeing the pretty birds and flowers,
And windmills with their sails and towers,
And all the wide sweep of the downs,
And villages and country towns,
And hear the mowers mowing hay,
And smell the great sea far away!
And always keeping – cars be blowed! –
Well on the wrong side of the road,
And never heeding hoots nor warners,
Especially around the corners,
For even down the steepest hill
Redemption saves me from a spill.

I have a flapper on my carrier
And some day I am going to marry her.

E. V. KNOX

Another Sad Shropshire Lad

When last I walked from Ludlow
The night was fine and clear:
I counted all them Severn stars
Through my parting glass of beer:
(It was so thin and dear).

Now I've been dead a fortnight
In lime instead of grass:
My horoscope was always bad,
Judge said I croaked my lass.
(I hanged at Michaelmas).

I cannot say who done it,
Though I did not, by drap:
But they harnessed me and trussed me,
And dropped me through a trap.
(This means I took the rap).

Some Shrewsbury spiv, I'll warrant,
It was as slit her throat:
But I'm the one as swung it
And me not worth a groat.
(I feel a silly goat).

A. G. PRYS-JONES

Morning Song

(AFTER SHAKESPEARE-SCHUBERT)

Horch, horch, die Bell am Backdoor ringt!
Get up! Es iss das Ice.
Ich hoff der Crook von Iceman bringt
A Piece von decent size.
Denn dass gibt shure a Scorcher heut,
Ich fühl alreddy heiss.
Und schlam die Shcreen-thür gut und tight,
Das Haus wird voll mit Flies.
Arise! Arise!
Eh's melten tut, arise!

KURT M. STEIN

Vor a Gauguin Picture zu Singen

Tahiti, Tahiti,[1]
Tahiti, Tahiti,
Sieh die Cocoa Cuties, mitaus noddings an.
Hier a Leaf, da a Leaf,
Hinten a Coral Reef.
Dass iss doch kein Climate für a mittelaged Mann.

KURT M. STEIN

1. Vamp until ready.

Translations from the Ish

THE CHARMING UNEXPECTED

When I find myself suddenly
Saying the right thing,
I feel like one whose dull-looking taxi-driver
Suddenly produces
(On being missed by a coal-cart)
A flow of language, noble,
Staggering,
Beautiful,
And checking all response.

MANUFACTURED EVIDENCE

Late in life,
Wishing to provide himself with a lurid past,
He had his chest tattooed with
Various
Regrettable
Designs.

SOUVENIR

'She was', said the young man, sniffing,
'The most beautiful girl
I ever saw.
For two minutes
I stood beside her
In a Tube lift.
I shall never see her again.
She gave me this cold.'

He sneezed with gloomy satisfaction,
And I noticed
That he had chosen to sit in a draught.

STATESMANSHIP

'Of course', said the leader of the Gadarene swine,
Rushing furiously towards the sea,
'One knows
That the rest don't really want
To come over this steep place.
But what can one do?
'I often wonder', he went on, panting,
'How we were manoeuvred
Into this position.'

THOUGHTS ON A SILENT AUDIENCE

I wish the people
Who think this comedian funny
(And numbers of them
Look the sort who might)
Would muster the energy to laugh,
And so allow me
To feel superior in comfort.

RECURRENT PROBLEM

Annually at certain seasons
I am moved during a meal
To question actuaries.

When I find an insect
In a vegetable
Are the odds in favour of, or against,
My finding another?

RICHARD MALLETT

Smith Minor Breaks a School Rule

'Boys are forbidden to let off fireworks on the School premises or in the
playground.' – Any Headmaster at the beginning of November.

By yong *Desire* importunate compell'd
(Him selfe not unconsenting) he procur'd
The seasonable store: bespangled Rod
With pouder al compact, or what beside
Of slender Shaft, or Wheele, or tortur'd Fuse
Reveal'd the maker's art. Awhile releas'd
From arduous Toyle, he o're the swarthy Plaine
To recreation dedicate and idle Playe,
Asphalt, the igneous Ore of antient Fyr,
His eger steps pursu'd. Him to prevent
The tedious Darkness, eldest Childe of Night,
The crafty Serpent with deceatful guile,
Perswading, he the convoluted Shape
Deep in his outward Vestment erst conceal'd
Brought forth incontinent. From ev'ry side
His watchful peers come flocking, busie Tongues
And curious Eies intent, about to see
The fiery Toye. So he the vital Sparke
From midget Rod with ardent Phosphor touch'd
With carefull Hand apply'd. Nor long delaies
Th' inevitable end; with mimic roare,
Now here, now there, the quick explosive Tube
Twixt fearfull feet pursues its errant waye.
Lone in his high and solitarie Seat,
Jove hears the Sound, and the auxiliar gods,
From reeking Herbe and steamy Nectar rous'd,
With list'ning Eares admire. Unfriended hee,
Helpless, alone, by some inferior Pow'r
In open Guilt arraign'd, with trembling Heart
Expects the coming Doom. . . .

                                        G. A. VALLINS

Alfred, Lord Tennyson rashly Contemplates a Morning Dip

xxxix

Rise up, O bright and tranquil Sun,
    And touch the wave with glowing fire,
    That outward deed and weak desire,
Too long disjoin'd, may be as one.

Rise up beyond the eastern hill
    And burn along the margent sea:
    Rise up, O Sun, and wake in me
The stern resolve, the iron will;

Rise up, in rich abundance pour
    Thy genial warmth from yonder sky;
    Outspread thy fiery beams, that I,
Delaying long, delay no more.

xl

Thou com'st, much look'd for; yet a breeze
    Shivers the dawn: the waters meet
    About my still reluctant feet,
And upward surge about my knees.

Uncertain, on the brink I stand
    Like ice, and turn my wistful eyes
    Backward, where in the sunlight lies
The safe and comfortable land.

No more; from out the swirling foam,
    The moaning of the mighty main,
    The deep that beckons me in vain,
A warmer prospect calls me home.

I dress; beside the distant sea
  I hear a voice cry 'All is well',
    And know that somewhere in The Bell
The coffee steams, and waits for me.

G. H. VALLINS

Sonnet

'Scorn not the sonnet. . . .' – WORDSWORTH: *Sonnets*

Scorn not the sonnet on the sonnet, critic;
  It is a bank where poets love to lie
  And praise each other's ingenuity
In finding such a form. The analytic
Reader may stigmatize as parasitic
  The mirror-image of a mystery,
  This echo of lost voices, find it dry
And intellectually paralytic.

Yet 'tis a child of Fancy, light and live,
  A fragile veil of Nature, scarcely worn
(Of Wordsworth's two, of Shakespeare's none, survive)
Empty not then the vials of scorn upon it.
  Nor, since we're on the subject, should you scorn
The sonnet on the sonnet on the sonnet.

PETER DICKINSON

BALLADS TO HARP ACCOMPANIMENT

Martin said to his Man

Martin said to his man,
     Fie, man! Fie!
O, Martin said to his man,
     Who's the foole now?
Martin said to his man,
Fill thou the cup and I the can,
Thou hast well drunken, man,
     Who's the foole now?

I see a sheep shearing corne,
     Fie, man! Fie!
I see a sheep shearing corne,
     Who's the foole now?
I see a sheep shearing corne,
And a cuckold blow his horn:
Thou hast well drunken, man,
     Who's the foole now?

I see a man in the moone;
     Fie, man! Fie!
I see a man in the moone,
     Who's the foole now?
I see a man in the moone,
Clowting of St Peter's shoone;
Thou hast well drunken, man,
     Who's the foole now?

I see a hare chase a hound,
     Fie, man! Fie!
I see a hare chase a hound,
     Who's the foole now?
I see a hare chase a hound
Twenty mile above the ground:

Thou hast well drunken, man,
    Who's the foole now?

I see a goose ring a hog,
    Fie, man! Fie!
I see a goose ring a hog,
    Who's the foole now?
I see a goose ring a hog
And a snayle that did bite a frog.
Thou hast well drunken, man,
    Who's the foole now?

I see a mouse catch a cat,
    Fie, man! Fie!
I see a mouse catch a cat.
    Who's the foole now?
I see a mouse catch a cat
And the cheese to eat the rat;
Thou hast well drunken, man,
    Who's the foole now?

ANON.

The Maid's Longing

A maiden of late
    Whose name was Sweet Kate,
She dwelt in London near Aldersgate;
    Now list to my ditty, declare it I can,
    She would have a child without help of a man.

To a doctor she came,
    A man of great fame,
Whose deep skill in physick report did proclaim.
    Quoth she: 'Mr Doctor, shew me if you can
    How I may conceive without help of a man.'

'Then listen,' quoth he,
'Since it must be,
This wondrous strange med'cine I'll shew presently;
Take nine pound of thunder, six legs of a swan,
And you shall conceive without help of a man.

'The love of false harlots,
The faith of false varlets,
With the truth of decoys that walk in their scarlet,
And the feathers of a lobster, well fry'd in a pan,
And you shall conceive without help of a man.

'Nine drops of rain
Brought hither from Spain,
With the blast of a bellows quite over the main,
With eight quarts of brimstone brew'd in a can,
And you shall conceive without help of a man.

'Six pottles of lard,
Squeez'd from rock hard,
With nine turkey eggs, each as long as a yard,
With pudding of hailstones well bak'd in a pan,
And you shall conceive without help of a man.

'These med'cines are good,
And approved have stood,
Well temper'd together with a pottle of blood
Squeez'd from a grasshopper and the nail of a swan,
To make maids conceive without help of a man.'

ANON.

The Crocodile

Now listen you landsmen unto me, to tell you the truth I'm bound,
What happened to me by going to sea, and the wonders that I
    found;
Shipwrecked I was once off Perouse and cast upon the shore,
So then I did resolve to roam, the country to explore.
    Tomy rit fal lal li bollem tit, tommy rit fal lal li dee!
    Tomy rit fal lal li bollem tit, tommy rit fal lal li dee!

'Twas far I had not scouted out, when close alongside the ocean,
I saw something move which at first I thought was all the world in
    motion;
But steering up close alongside, I found 'twas a crocodile,
And from his nose to the tip of his tail he measured five hundred
    mile.
    Tomy rit, etc.

When up aloft the wind was high, it blew a gale from the south,
I lost my hold and away did fly right into the crocodile's mouth,
He quickly closed his jaws on me and thought he'd got a victim,
But I ran down his throat, d'ye see, and that's the way I tricked him.
    Tomy rit, etc.

I travelled on for a month or two, till I got into his maw,
Where I found of rum-kegs not a few, and a thousand fat bullocks
    in store,
Of life I banished all my care, for of grub I was not stinted,
And in this crocodile I lived ten years, and very well contented.
    Tomy rit, etc.

This crocodile being very old, one day, alas, he died;
He was ten long years a-getting cold, he was so long and wide.
His skin was eight mile thick, I'm sure, or very near about,
For I was ten years or more a cutting my way out.
    Tomy rit, etc.

And now I've once more got on earth, I've vow'd no more to roam,
In a ship that passed I got a berth, and now I'm safe at home,
And if my story you should doubt, should you ever travel the Nile,
It's ten to one you'll find the shell of the wonderful crocodile.

    Tomy rit, etc.

ANON.

Here's the Man A-coming!

In Lunnon town each day, strange sayings will be springing,
But, if you list to me, a new one I'll be singing,
As you go through the town, the people will be funning,
One cries out, 'Put it down, here's the man a-coming!'

'Twas only t'other day, as sure as I'm a sinner,
A leg of pork I bought, to have a slap-up dinner;
When, half way down the street, a young scamp came by, running,
Says he, 'Guvner, drop that meat, here's the man a-coming!'

Young married folks, I fear, to extremes often dash on,
They're always in a fright, through studying the fashion;
Each day with fear and dread, the tradesmen they are shunning.
'Jem, get under the bed, here's the tally man a-coming!'

There's lots of ups and downs, and lots of rummy dodgings,
But I do it quite brown, in taking furnish'd lodgings;
I own I'm very poor, to pay there is no fun in,
So I always bolt the door when I hear the landlord coming!

It's pleasant, in this place, to see your smiling faces.
And, gents, too, I presume, you're in your proper places;
Now, there's one stands there so sly, I know he's very cunning,
I say, 'Mind what you're at, here's the man a-coming!'

ANON.

The Lord Mayor's Show

How well I remember the ninth of November,
The Sky very foggy, the Sun looking groggy,
In fact, altogether pea-soup colour's weather.
Shop-windows all shutter'd, the pavement all butter'd,
Policemen paraded, the street barricaded,
  And a peal from the steeple of Bow!
Low women in pattens, high ladies in satins,
And Cousin Suburbans, in flame-colour'd turbans,
Quite up to the attics, inviting rheumatics,
A great mob collecting, without much selecting,
And some, it's a pity, are free of the city,
  As your pockets may happen to know! ...

Such hustle and bustle, and mobbing and robbing,
All, all to see the Lord May'r's Show!

How well I remember the ninth of November,
Six trumpets on duty, as shrill as Veluti,
A great City Marshal, to riding not partial,
The footmen, the state ones, with calves very great ones,
The Cook and the Scullion, well basted with bullion,
  And the squad of each Corporate Co.
Four draymen from Perkins, in steel and brass jerkins,
A Coach like a lantern, I wonder it *can* turn,
All carved like old buildings, and drawn by six *gildings*,
With two chubby faces, where sword and where mace is,
The late May'r, the Ex one, a thought that must vex one,
  And the new May'r just come into blow!

Such hustle and bustle, and mobbing and robbing,
All, all to see the Lord May'r's Show.

How well I remember the ninth of November,
The fine Lady May'ress, an Ostrich's heiress,
In best bib and tucker, and dignified pucker,

The learned Recorder, in Old Bailey order,
The Sheriffs together, – with their hanging weather,
    And their heads like John Anderson's pow!
The Aldermen courtly, and looking 'red port'ly,
And buckler and bargemen, with other great large men,
With streamers and banners, held up in odd manners,
A mob running 'arter', to see it by 'vater',
    And the Wharfs popping off as they go! ...

Such hustle and bustle, such mobbing and robbing,
All, all to see the Lord May'r's Show!

THOMAS HOOD

The Cadger's Ball

Oh, what a spicy flare-up, tear-up,
    Festival Terpsickory,
Was guv'd by the genteel cadgers
    In the famous Rookery.
As soon as it got vind, however,
    Old St Giles's vos to fall –
They all declar'd, so help their never,
    They'd vind up vith a stunnin' ball!
        Tol, lol, lol, etc.

Jack Flipflap took the affair in hand, sirs –
    Who understood the thing complete –
He'd often danced afore the public,
    On the boards, about the streets,
Old Mother Swankey, she consented
    To lend her lodging-house for nix –
Says she, 'The crib comes down tomorrow,
    So go it, just like beans and bricks.'
        Tol, lol, lol, etc.

The night arrived for trotter-shaking –
 To Mother Swankey's snoozing-crib;
Each downy cadger was seen taking
 His bit of muslin, or his rib.
Twelve candles vos stuck into turnips,
 Suspended from the ceiling queer –
Bunn's blaze of triumph was all pickles
 To this wegetable shandileer.
  Tol, lol, lol, etc.

Ragged Jack, wot chalks 'Starvation!'
 Look'd quite fat and swellish there –
While Dick, wot 'dumbs it' round the nation,
 Had all the jaw among the fair.
Limping Ned, wot brought his duchess,
 At home had left his wooden pegs –
And Jim, wot cadges it on crutches,
 Vos the nimblest covey on his legs.
  Tol, lol, lol, etc.

The next arrival was old Joe Burn,
 Wot does the fits to Natur chuff –
And Fogg, wot's blind each day in Ho'born,
 Saw'd his way there clear enough,
Mr Sinniwating Sparrow,
 In corduroys span new and nice,
Druv up in his pine-apple barrow,
 Which he used to sell a win a slice.
  Tol, lol, lol, etc.

The ball was open'd by fat Mary,
 Togg'd out in book muslin pure,
And Saucy Sam, surnamed, 'The Lary',
 Who did the *Minuit-on-a-squre.*
While Spifflicating Charley Coker,
 And Jane of the hatchet-face divine,

Just did the Rowdydowdy Poker,
   And out of Greasy took the shine.
      Tol, lol, lol, etc.

The Sillywarious next was done in
   Tip-top style, just as it should,
By Muster and Missus Mudfog, stunning,
   Whose hair curled like a bunch of wood.
The fols grinn'd all about their faces,
   'Cos Mudfog – prince of flashy bucks –
Had on a pair of pillow Cases
   Transmogrified slap into ducks!
      Tol, lol, lol, etc.

The celebrated Pass de Sandwich
   To join in no one could refuse –
Six bushels on 'em came in, and wich
   Wanish'd in about two two's.
The Gatter Waltz next followed arter –
   They lapp'd it down right manful-ly,
Until Joe Guffin and his darter,
   Was in a state of Fourpen-ny!
      Tol, lol, lol, etc.

Next came the Pass de Fascination
   Betwixt Peg Price and Dumby Dick –
But Peg had sich a corporation,
   He dropp'd her like a red hot brick.
The company was so enraptur'd,
   They *buckets* of vall flowers threw –
But one chap flung a bunch of turnips,
   Which nearly split Dick's nut in two.
      Tol, lol, lol, etc.

The dose now set to gallopading,
   And stamp'd with all their might and main –

They thump'd the floor so precious hard-in,
    It split the ancient crib in twain,
Some pitch'd in the road, bent double –
    Some was smash'd with bricks – done brown –
So the cadgers saved 'The Crown' the trouble
    Of sending coves to pull it down.
            Tol, lol, lol, etc.

                        ANON.

Blow Me Eyes!

When I was young and full o' pride,
    A-standin' on the grass
And gazin' o'er the water-side,
    I seen a fisher lass.
'O fisher-lass, be kind awhile,'
    I asks 'er quite unbid.
'Please look into me face and smile' –
    And blow me eyes, she did!

O blow me light, and blow me blow,
I didn't think she'd charm me so –
    But, blow me eyes, she did!

She seemed so young and beautiful
    I *had* to speak perlite,
(The afternoon was long and dull,
    But she was short and bright).
'This ain't no place', I says, 'to stand –
    Let's take a walk instid,
Each holdin' of the other's hand' –
    And, blow me eyes, she did!

O, blow me light and blow me blow,
I sort o' thunk she wouldn't go –
    But, blow me eyes, she did!

As we walked along a lane
   With no one else to see,
My heart was filled with sudden pain,
   And so I says to she:
'If you would have me actions speak
   The words what can't be hid,
You'd sort o' let me kiss yer cheek' —
   And, blow me eyes, she did!

O, blow me light and blow me blow,
How sweet she was I didn't know —
   But, blow me eyes, *she* did!

But pretty soon me shipmate Jim
   Came strollin' down the beach,
And she began a-oglin' him
   As pretty as a peach.
'O fickle maid o' false intent,'
   Impulsively I chid,
'Why don't you go and wed that gent?'
   And, blow me eyes, she did!

O, blow me light and blow me blow,
I didn't think she'd treat me so —
   But, blow me eyes, she did!

WALLACE IRWIN

Unhappy Bella

Bella was young and Bella was fair
With bright blue eyes and golden hair,
O unhappy Bella!
Her step was light and her heart was gay,
But she had no sense and one fine day
She got herself put in the family way
By a wicked, heartless, cruel deceiver.

Poor Bella was young, she didn't believe
That the world is hard and men deceive,
O unhappy Bella!
She said, 'My man will do what's just,
He'll marry me now, because he must';
Her heart was full of loving trust
In a wicked, heartless, cruel deceiver.

She went to his house; that dirty skunk
Had packed his bags and done a bunk,
O unhappy Bella!
Her landlady said, 'Get out, you whore,
I won't have your sort a-darkening my door.'
Poor Bella was put to affliction sore
By a wicked, heartless, cruel deceiver.

All night she tramped the cruel snows,
What she must have suffered nobody knows,
O unhappy Bella!
And when the morning dawned so red,
Alas, alas, poor Bella was dead,
Sent so young to her lonely bed
By a wicked, heartless, cruel deceiver.

So thus, you see, do what you will,
The fruits of sin are suffering still,
O unhappy Bella!
As into the grave they laid her low,
The men said, 'Alas, but life is so,'
But the women chanted, sweet and low,
'It's all the men, the dirty bastards!'

ANON.

Mule

My Mammy was a wall-eyed goat,
My Old Man was an ass,
And I feed myself off leather boots
And dynamite and grass;
For I'm a mule, a long-eared fool
And I ain't never been to school —
  Mammeee! Ma-ha-mam-hee!
  Heee-haw! Mamaah!
  Ma-ha-mee!

ANON.

Not Tonight, Josephine

Though I have an admiration for your charming resignation
(There appears no limitation to your constant animation)
And a deep appreciation of your warm cooperation,
And I find a consolation in the pleasing contemplation
Of a coy anticipation quite beyond articulation,
Yet forgive the implication if I plead disinclination
For the sweet exhilaration of a brief amalgamation.
I'll tell you in a phrase, my sweet, exactly what I mean:
  ... Not tonight, Josephine.

COLIN CURZON

SHORT MEASURE

AUGUSTAN MALICE

On an Empty House

Lollus, by night awak'd, heard thieves about
His house, and searching narrowly throughout
To find some pillage there, he said: 'You may,
By night, but I can find naught there by day.'

ANON.

Woman

A *Woman* is a book, and often found
To prove far better in the Sheets than bound:
No marvel then why men take such delight
Above all things to *study in the night*.

ANON.

To a Covetous Woman who Rouged her Cheeks while recovering from the Yellow Jaundice

Ungrateful Slave of Gold! What, *blush* to be
The wearer of *your master's livery!*

ANON.

On a Musician and Dancing-Master who Decamped with Cash subscribed for a Musical Publication

His *time* was quick, his *touch* was fleet;
  Our gold he neatly *finger'd:*
Alike alert with *hand* and *feet*,
  His *movements* have not linger'd.
Where lies the wonder of the case?
  A moment's thought detects it:

His practice has been *thorough-bass*,
  A *chord* will be his exit.
Yet, while we blame his hasty flight,
  Our censure may be rash.
A traveller is surely right
  To change his *notes* for cash.

ANON.

From the French

Dennis, an author cold and weak,
  Thinks as a critic he's divine;
Likely enough – we often make
  Good vinegar of sorry wine.

LINGO

On a Pale Lady with a Red-Nosed Husband

Whence comes it that in Clara's face
  The lily only has its place?
Is it because the absent rose
  Has gone to paint her husband's nose?

ANON.

Written on a Looking Glass

I change, and so do women too;
But I reflect, which women never do.

ANON.

The Wife's Epitaph

To follow you I'm not content.
How do I know which way you went?

ANON.

To –

Money's like muck, that's profitable while
'T serves for manuring of some fruitful soil;
But on a barren one, like thee, methinks,
'Tis like a dunghill that lies still and stinks.

RICHARD FLECKNOE

An Empty House

You beat your pate, and fancy wit will come:
Knock as you please, there's nobody at home.

ALEXANDER POPE

Verses on the 4th of November

Tonight's the night, I speak it with great sorrow,
That we were all to have been blown up tomorrow;
Therefore take care of fires and candle-light,
'Tis a cold frosty morning, and so good-night.

An Impromptu by the BEADLE OF ST PATRICK'S
(reported by Jonathan Swift)

His last great Debt is paid – poor Tom's no more.
Last Debt! Tom never paid a debt before.

ANON.

Charles, grave or merry, at no lie would stick,
And taught at length his memory the same trick.
Believing thus what he so oft repeats,
He's brought the thing to such a pass, poor youth,
    That now himself and no one else he cheats,
Save when unluckily he tells the truth.

ANON.

From the German of Lessing

You hesitate if you shall take a wife.
Do as your father did – live single all your life.

ANON.

To a Lawyer

Trapped by my neighbour in his clover,
Three pigs I fee'd you to recover.
Before the court you gravely stand,
And stroke your wig and smooth your band;
Then, taking up the kingdom's story,
You ope your case with Alfred's glory;
Of Norman William's curfew bell
And Coeur de Lion's prowess tell;
How through the ravaged fields of France
Edwards and Henries shook the lance;
How great Eliza o'er the main
Pursu'd the shatter'd pride of Spain,
And Orange broke a tyrant's claim.
　　All this, good sir, is mighty fine;
But now, an please you, to my swine!

ANON.

Ned calls his wife his counter-part
　　With truth as well as whim;
Since every impulse of her heart
　　Runs counter still to him.

ANON.

On a Wrestler

Death to the Wrestler gave a pretty fall,
Tript up his heels, and took no hold at all.

ANON.

Such a liar is Ned that there's none can lie faster,
Excepting his maid, and she'll lie with her master.

ANON.

On Morcho

Morcho for haste was married in the night.
What needed day? His fair young wife is light.

ANON.

On a Lady who Beat her Husband

Come hither, Sir John, my picture is here.
  What think you, my love, don't it strike you?
I can't say it does just at present, my dear,
  But I think it soon will, it's so like you.

ANON.

Gallus hath got a widow wondrous old,
The reason is he woo'd her for her gold:
Knowing her maids are young and serve for hire,
Which is as much as Gallus doth desire.

ANON.

When the devil engaged with Job's patience in battle,
Tooth and nail strove to weary him out of his life,
He robb'd him of children, slaves, houses, and cattle,
But, mark me – he ne'er thought of taking his wife,

But Heaven, at length, Job's forbearance rewards;
At length double wealth, double honour arrives;
Heaven doubles his children, slaves, houses and herds –
But we don't hear a word of a *couple of wives*.

ANON.

When I call'd you a blockhead, I candidly own
It was hastily done, for I could not have shown
   Such proof as would warrant conviction:
But, thanks to the anger my boldness has raised,
You're an author become, and now, Fortune be prais'd,
   I've proof that defies contradiction.

R. A. D.

(from the French of Fabian Pillet)

On John Dove, Innkeeper, Mauchline

    Here lies Johnnie Pigeon;
    What was his religion,
       Whe'er desires to ken,
    To some other warl
    Maun follow the carl,
       For here Johnnie Pigeon had nane.

    Strong ale was ablution,
    Small beer persecution,
       A dram was *memento mori;*
    But a full flowing bowl
    Was the saving his soul,
       And port was celestial glory.

ROBERT BURNS

    We men have many faults.
       Poor women have but two:—
    There's nothing good they say;
    There's nothing good they do.

ANON.

Inscribed on a Pint-Pot

There are several reasons for drinking,
And one has just entered my head;
If a man cannot drink when he's living
How the Hell can he drink when he's dead?

ANON.

On a Vicious Person

He called thee vicious, did he? lying elf!
Thou art not vicious; thou art vice itself.

FLETCHER

I shudder if perchance I meet
Long-winded Dromio in the street,
For surely no man living says
So little in so tedious phrase.
Dromio, it seems, is doomed by fate
On nothing evermore to prate: —
But destiny, by the same decree,
Assigns a heavier lot to me;
Me, who, whenever I come near him
Am doomed eternally to hear him

SAMUEL BISHOP

A Bon Mot

ON A LADY'S WEDDING BEING ON THE 21ST OF DECEMBER

Return'd from the opera, as lately I sat,
Indifferently chatting of this and of that,
My Chloe I asked how it entered her head
To fix on St Thomas, of all days to wed
To which she replied, with reason the strongest,
'Tho' shortest the day is — the night, sir, is longest.'

VAUGHAN

On Ale

Of this strange drink, so like the Stygian lake,
Which men call Ale, I know not what to make.
Folk drink it thick and void it very thin.
Therefore much dregs must needs remain within.

ANON.

John sobbed and whimpered when he saw
His wife lie squalling in the straw;
'I suffer much', quoth she, ''tis true;
But don't weep, John – I don't blame you.'

E. WALSH

In vino veritas, they say,
    Yet lying is so much the custom
Of certain folk, the safest way
    Is, drunk or sober, not to trust 'em.

ANON.

Tom found a trinket in his bed,
Which he'd to Stephen's mistress given:
'What's this, dear wife?' – 'Only (she said)
Your *gift* to *Ann* – returned by Stephen.'

ANON.

On Seeing a Lady's Garter

Why blush, dear girl, pray tell me why?
    You need not, I can prove it;
For though your garter met my eye,
    My thoughts were far above it.

ANON.

Epigram

Some Men of Books are wond'rous nice
In buying all that's rare and choice; —
Now Maevius, on a different plan,
Buys up the veriest trash he can,
And hoards, with avaricious glee,
His huge waste-paper library
In garrets, sheds and lofts for hay,
Till tons of learning mould away: —
Mourn ye cook-shops and common sewers,
The loss, alack, is wholly *yours!*

ANON.

A hamper I received of wine,
As good, Dick says, as ere was tasted —
And Dick may be supposed to know,
For he contriv'd his matters so
As every day with me to dine
Much longer than the liquor lasted: —
If such are presents — while I live,
Oh, let me not receive — but give!

(imitated from the French)
P. DODD

On Dorinda's Fore-teeth

OCCASIONED BY HER DENYING THE AUTHOR A KISS

No more, Dorinda, scorn the Bliss,
Thro' vain mistaken Pride:
The Profit's yours; for when we kiss,
Your Teeth a-while we hide.

ANON.

Jack, eating rotten cheese, did say;
'Like Samson I my thousands slay':
'I vow', quoth Roger, 'so you do,
And with the self-same weapon too.'

ANON.

Upon a Company of Bad Dancers to Good Musick

How ill the Motion with the Musick suits!
So *Orpheus* fiddles, and so danc'd the Brutes.

ANON.

Belinda has such wondrous charms
'Tis heaven to be within her arms;
And she's so charitably given
She wishes all mankind in heaven.

THOMAS WALTHOE

On Taking a Wife

'Come, come,' said Tom's father, 'at your time of life,
There's no longer excuse for thus playing the rake.
It's time you should think, boy, of taking a wife.'
'Why so it is, father. Whose wife shall I take?'

THOMAS MOORE

Epitaph

Posterity will ne'er survey
A nobler grave than this:
Here lie the bones of Castlereagh:
Stop, traveller, *** ****.

GEORGE GORDON, LORD BYRON

Epitaph on John Adams of Southwell
A CARRIER WHO DIED OF DRUNKENNESS

John Adams lies here, of the parish of Southwell,
A *Carrier* who *carried* his can to his mouth well;
He *carried* so much and he *carried* so fast,
He could *carry* no more – so was *carried* at last;
For the liquor he drank, being too much for one,
He could not *carry off*; so he's now *carry-on*.

GEORGE GORDON, LORD BYRON

Epitaph on Meredith Morgan

Under this stone lies Meredith Morgan,
Who blew the bellows of our church organ.
Tobacco he hated; to smoke most unwilling,
Yet never so pleased as when *pipes* he was filling.
No reflection on him for rude speech could be cast,
Tho' he made our church organ give many a *blast*.
No *puffer* was he tho' a *capital* blower,
He could fill double C, and now lies a note lower.

ANON.

Epitaph

Here lies a man who was killed by lightning;
He died when his prospects seemed to be brightening.
He might have cut a flash in this world of trouble,
But the flash cut him, and he lies in the stubble.

ANON.

Here lies Pat Steel,
   That's very true.
Who was he? what was he?
   What is that to you?

ANON.

An Epitaph

A lovely young lady I mourn in my rhymes:
She was pleasant, good-natured and civil sometimes.
Her figure was good: she had very fine eyes,
And her talk was a mixture of foolish and wise.
Her adorers were many, and one of them said,
'She waltzed rather well! It's a pity she's dead!'

G. J. CAYLEY

The Bishop's Last Directions

Tell my Priests, when I am gone,
O'er me to shed no tears,
For I shall be no deader then
Than they have been for years.

ANON.

Epigram

After such years of dissension and strife,
Some wonder that Peter should weep for his wife:
But his tears on her grave are nothing surprising, –
He's laying her dust, for fear of its rising.

THOMAS HOOD

'To this night's masquerade,' quoth Dick,
  By pleasure I am beckon'd,
And think 'twould be a pleasant trick
  To go as Charles the Second.'

Tom felt for repartee a thirst,
  And thus to Richard said: –
'You'd better go as Charles the First,
  For that requires no head.'

HORACE SMITH

ROMANTIC NONSENSE

The Herring

The Herring he loves the merry moonlight
   And the Mackerel loves the wind,
But the Oyster loves the dredging song
   For he comes of a gentler kind.

SIR WALTER SCOTT

On the Death of the Giraffe

They say, God wot,
She died upon the spot:
But then in spots she was so rich, —
I wonder which?

THOMAS HOOD

'Tis Midnight

'Tis midnight, and the setting sun
   Is slowly rising in the west;
The rapid rivers slowly run,
   The frog is on his downy nest.
The pensive goat and sportive cow,
Hilarious, leap from bough to bough.

ANON.

An Unsuspected Fact

If down his throat a man should choose,
In fun, to jump or slide,
He'd scrape his shoes against his teeth,
Nor dirt his own inside.

But if his teeth were lost and gone,
And not a stump to scrape upon,
He'd see at once how very pat
His tongue lay there by way of mat,
And he would wipe his feet on *that!*

EDWARD CANNON

Two Aboriginal Poems

Chackaboo, chickaboo, chuckaboo, chew,
Mark baby over with pretty tattoo;
Cut in the pattern like openwork tart:
Rub in the powder and make baby smart.

*

What, cry when I cook you, not like to be stewed?
Then go and be raw, and not fit to be food.
Until you leave off, and I see that you've smiled,
I shan't take the trouble to eat such a child.

SHIRLEY BROOKS

Here's a little proverb that you surely ought to know:
Horses sweat and men perspire, but ladies only glow.

ANON.

King David and King Solomon
    Led merry, merry lives,
With many, many lady friends
    And many, many wives;
But when old age crept over them,
    With many, many qualms,
King Solomon wrote the Proverbs,
    And King David wrote the Psalms.

J. B. NAYLOR

Consolatory

Neighbour Nickle feels downcast
And has every reason to,
For of all his plans at last
Every one has fallen through.

Jill our nanny-goat has died.
Go and tell him quickly, boy!
Long and sorely he's been tried:
Why begrudge him one small joy?

WILHELM BUSCH
(translated by MICHAEL HAMBURGER)

Over their pints they made much fuss
  About Charles Darwin's theory;
The very thought was ludicrous,
  Not to speak of human dignity.

They emptied many a tankard there
  And staggered out of doors;
Each grunted audibly as up the stair
  He crawled upon all fours.

WILHELM BUSCH
(translated by MICHAEL HAMBURGER)

To the Moon

Oh Moon, when I look on thy beautiful face,
Careering along through the boundaries of space,
The thought has quite frequently come to my mind,
If ever I'll gaze on thy glorious behind.

ANON.

The Sun!

The sun's perpendicular rays
Illumine the depths of the sea;
The fishes, beginning to sweat,
Cried: 'Damn it, how hot we shall be!'

W. L. MANSEL

Teach not thy parent's mother to extract
The embryo juices of the bird by suction.
The good old lady can that feat enact
Quite irrespective of the kind instruction.

ANON.

3

THREE LIMERICKS

A simple young fellow named Hyde
In a funeral procession was spied.
   When asked, 'Who is dead?'
   He tittered and said,
'I don't know. I just came for the ride.'

ANON.

There was an old man from Darjeeling,
Who boarded a bus bound for Ealing.
   He saw on the door:
   'Please don't spit on the floor',
So he stood up and spat on the ceiling.

ANON.

There was an old man of Khartoum
Who kept a tame sheep in his room.
'To remind me', he said,
'Of someone who's dead,
But I never can recollect whom'.

ANON.

4

A BUNCH OF CLERIHEWS

The Empress Poppaea
Was really rather a dear,
Only no one could stop her
From being improper.

ANON.

Cecil B. de Mille,
Rather against his will,
Was persuaded to leave Moses
Out of 'The Wars of the Roses'.

NICOLAS BENTLEY

The Emperor Arcadius
Lived outside the four-mile radius,
Which made it rather laborious
To visit the Emperor Honorius.

ANON.

Geoffrey Chaucer
Always drank out of a saucer.
He said it made him feel such an ass
To drink out of a glass.

ANON.

Diodorus Siculus
Made himself ridiculous.
He thought a thimble
Was the phallic symbol.

ANON.

Jonathan Swift
Never went up in a lift;
Nor did the author of 'Robinson Crusoe'
Do so.

ANON.

Abraham Lincoln
Never read the 'Pink 'un';
He preferred
God's Word.

E. K. BENNETT

On British Films

Isn't it funny
How they never make any money,
While everyone *in* the racket
Cleans up such a packet?

J. B. BOOTHROYD

5

MORE OR LESS TOPICAL

Weather Forecast

The Rain it raineth every day,
  Upon the just and unjust fellow,
But more upon the just, because
  The unjust has the just's umbrella.

ANON.

What is a Basket?

'Oh, Daddy dear, what is a basket?'
Said a youthful and mischievous elf:
'All baskets, me boy, are children of joy.
In fact you're a basket yourself.'

ANON.

Abey! Seed' Goldfish

A.B.C.D. Gol'fish?
M.N.O. Gol'fish.
S.D.R. Gol'fish.
R.D.R. Gol'fish.

ANON.

As I was laying on the green
A little book it chanced I seen.
Carlyle's *Essay on Burns* was the edition —
I left it laying in the same position.

ANON.

Fatigue

I'm tired of Love: I'm still more tired of Rhyme.
But Money gives me pleasure all the time.

HILAIRE BELLOC

Rollo Grows all Creepy Crowley

I saw you dining on the 14th ult.
At the *Two Snails* with such a curious creature.
You say she is the priestess of your cult?
She looked more like an unfrocked pupil-teacher.

E. POWYS MATHERS

Sui Prodigus

We constantly hear O'Flannagan say
  'I gave him a piece of my mind,'
Which is why, when so much has been given away,
  So little remains behind.

                              A. B. RAMSAY

Consecration

With lips alone MacAndrew sanctifies,
  A thing, it seems, is right because he's said it;
Still holier influence falls from Winkle's eyes;
  With him, a book is good because he's read it.

                              A. B. RAMSAY

Said Dickon, searching for the spring
  Of actual knowledge, 'Blow it!
I find that though I know a thing,
  I cannot know I know it.'

                              A. B. RAMSAY

H.B.

That rather jolly rum-looking man over there,
So kind to all and some, so warm and debonair,
As fat as a plum and as soft as a slug –
His Christian name is Hum, and his surname is Bug.

                              A. B. RAMSAY

Sibi Constans

You always say 'I always say –'
At any hour on any day,
By every gust of doctrine blown,
Consistent yet in this alone.

So might a spinning weather-cock
Keep crowing 'I am like a rock'
And, boxing all the compass, cry
'Nought so immoveable as I'.

And men shall say when you are dead,
'There's nothing that he always said
Except that, any hour or day,
He always said, "I always say".'

A. B. RAMSAY

Epitaph on a Syndic

No teacher I of boys or smaller fry,
No teacher I of teachers, no, not I.
Mine was the distant aim, the longer reach,
To teach men how to teach men how to teach.

A. B. RAMSAY

Carelessness

A window-cleaner in our street
Who fell (five storeys) at my feet
Impaled himself on my umbrella.
I said: 'Come, come, you careless fella!
If my umbrella had been shut
You might have landed on my nut.'

HARRY GRAHAM

Compensation

Weep not for little Léonie,
Abducted by a French *Marquis!*
Though loss of honour was a wrench,
Just think how it's improved her French.

HARRY GRAHAM

Mr Jones

'There's been an accident,' they said,
'Your servant's cut in half; he's dead!'
'Indeed!' said Mr Jones, 'and please
Send me the half that's got my keys.'

                                    HARRY GRAHAM

To a Lady Who wanted a Penny for Two Ha'pennies

Look lidy, foller Olive Snell,
To 'oom yore accident befell.
It 'appened, as it does to many,
That *Olive* went to spend a penny.

She searched 'er bag, and 'ad jist one –
An' that wus bent – so wot she done?
She went and found a spinney shidy. ...
An' saved 'erself the penny, lidy!

                                    ARNOLD SILCOCK

Three Epitaphs

Here lies a cannibal who, now and then,
Forgetting the advice of his physician,
Absorbed the deadliest poison known to men,
And died of politician.

*

Here lies Tobias, our dear cat,
Who breathed his last upon the mat,
His death was due to cook's mistake
In giving him our processed hake.
The moral's plain. It is no treat
For pets to have what humans eat.

*

Here lies the victim of experiment,
Hard by the byre she was the joy and pride of;
They played Valse Triste to make her more content,
Alas! That was the tune the old cow died of.

J. B. MORTON

Poem

(BASED ON AN OLD FRENCH PROVERB)

People who live in Chateaux
Shouldn't throw tomateaux.

J. B. MORTON

Song of the Ballet

Lift her up tenderly,
   Raise her with care,
Catch hold of one leg,
   And a handful of hair;
Swing her round savagely,
And when this palls,
Heave-Ho! Away with her
   Into the stalls.

J. B. MORTON

Footnote to Tennyson

I feel it when the game is done,
I feel it when I suffer most.
'Tis better to have loved and lost
Than ever to have loved and won.

GERALD BULLETT

So you'll to the Psychiatrist,
Your little psyche's queer?
You need, I think, to see a good
Psmackbottomist, my dear!

ANON.

Design for Misgivings

Monkeys romping in the Zoo
Shiver with a modest grue
When they hear their keeper say:
'Almost like a Coward play!'

D. B. WYNDHAM LEWIS

Envoi

I warmed both hands before the fire of Life,
I thought the heat and smoke were pretty swell;
Yet now I cannot cease from mental strife –
Should I have warmed my poor old feet as well?

D. B. WYNDHAM LEWIS

On Nevski Bridge a Russian stood
Chewing his beard for lack of food.
Said he, 'It's tough this stuff to eat
But a darn sight better than shredded wheat!'

ANON.

An accident happened to my brother Jim
When somebody threw a tomato at him –
Tomatoes are juicy and don't hurt the skin,
But this one was specially packed in a tin.

ANON.

Silver Lining

Cold is the night and chill the grate.
My Loved One fareth far and late.
My Loved One tarrieth late afar –
He hath a heater in the car.

JUSTIN RICHARDSON

Take Heart, Illiterates

AN EPIGRAM

For years a secret shame destroyed my peace —
I'd not read Eliot, Auden or MacNeice.
But now I think a thought that brings me hope:
Neither had Chaucer, Shakespeare, Milton, Pope.

JUSTIN RICHARDSON

The Goldfish

The gaping goldfish in his bowl
I'm sure is happy on the whole:
He has that silly vacant look
Because he's never read a book.

A. G. PRYS-JONES

Hippopotamus

The genial hippopotamus
Is not exactly one of us,
He does not smoke, or drink or cuss,
And is, I've heard, monogamous.

A. G. PRYS-JONES

The Vulture

The vulture
Is preoccupied with sepulture:
He doesn't find this at all gloomy
Because nature has built him adequately roomy.

A. G. PRYS-JONES

Eisteddfod Piece

'What is the matter with that Druid, Daddy?
Why is he whistling and limping so?'
'He's whistling to summon up his bardic spirit,
And he's probably got gout in his mistletoe.'

A. G. PRYS-JONES

Business as Usual

When Gabriel's starting trumpet rends the skies,
And all arise for that last race of man,
Dai Jones, the bookie, glasses to his eyes,
Will spot the winners, and the also ran.

A. G. PRYS-JONES

Useful Higher Education

A Harvard man named Wilbur Crats
Made a career of burgling flats:
But owed his prowess, so to speak,
Entirely to his Yale technique.

A. G. PRYS-JONES

Quite So

Within the whispering gallery of St Paul's
The merest whisper travels round the walls:
But in the parts where I was born and bred
Folk hear things long before they're even said.

A. G. PRYS-JONES

Ausland

The air is edged with ice and the sun's beam,
And melts in the mouth like ice-cream.
Every dog has his day, and cats have week-ends
In which to visit friends.

AUTHOR UNKNOWN

The Termite

Some primal termite knocked on wood
And tasted it, and found it good,
And that is why your Cousin May
Fell through the parlour floor today.

OGDEN NASH

The Perfect Husband

He tells you when you've got on
          too much lipstick
And helps you with your girdle
          when your hips stick.

OGDEN NASH

Reflection on Babies

A bit of talcum
Is always walcum.

OGDEN NASH

The Parent

Children aren't happy with nothing to ignore,
And that's what parents were created for.

OGDEN NASH

The Rhinoceros

The rhino is a homely beast,
For human eyes he's not a feast.
Farewell, farewell, you old rhinoceros,
I'll stare at something less prepoceros.

OGDEN NASH

The Persistence of Memory

FROM THE SPANISH OF A PICTURE BY SALVADOR DALI

Timepieces flow from table edge –
　Trick glutinous toward the shore
From blasted tree and what the dredge
　　Dragged up from sea's subconscious floor.
　　　Back of beyond runs out bright cliff
　　　Where time and times are frozen stiff.

GEOFFREY TAYLOR

Counter Attack

We talk of things you never thought quite nice.
　Your closet dream we speak with better grace;
All that we do now without thinking twice,
　You do or did with conscience-bitten face.
To keep the cup clean we keep clean the sink.
　My mote perhaps, Sir, but your beam, I think.

GEOFFREY TAYLOR

To a School Juliet

Could I forget you in that other play,
　Then might your gentleness command belief
Nor present scenes be dulled by yesterday –
　With recollection muddied o'er. ...
　　　　　　　In brief,
Sweet Capulet, I cannot overcome
The mem'ry of thee shoving in the scrum.

MARK BEVAN

Out of Sight, Out of Mind

My eyes floated out of their eyebaths
And wandered away down the street;
I watched with a certain detachment,
Then the thought slowly entered my brain —
My eyes will be having a wonderful time,
But I, shall I see them again?

ALAN CRICK

Muffle

As I was drinking muffled punch
And eating muffled eggs for lunch
I saw a man with muffled feet
Who sat upon a muffled seat
And then began with muffled eyes
To sing some muffled lullabies.
I don't believe I've ever been
At a more deeply muffled scene.

ALAN CRICK

Uncommon Sensibility

'He's so sensitive, poor fellow!' —
If you tread on his feet he'll bellow.
If he cracks your shin with his boot,
Why, he's deaf, he's blind and he's mute.

MICHAEL HAMBURGER

Auntie

Auntie always was morose
And her views on life were bitter,
For she was so adipose
No ordinary seat would fit'er:
Now I should think that you'd feel glum
If you'd been born with Auntie's sitter!

ANON.

AND FOUR FOR THE ROAD

The Beautiful Incendiary

BY THE HON. W. S.

Formosam resonare doces Amaryllida silvas – *Virgil.*

Scene draws, and discovers a Lady asleep on a couch
Enter Philander

PHILANDER

Sobriety, cease to be sober,
  Cease Labour, to dig and to delve;
All hail to this tenth of October,
  One thousand eight hundred and twelve!
Ha! whom do my peepers remark?
  'Tis Hebe with Jupiter's jug;
O no, 'tis the pride of the Park,
  Fair Lady Elizabeth Mugg.

Why, beautiful nymph, do you close
  The curtain that fringes your eye?
Why veil in the clouds of repose
  The sun that should brighten our sky?
Perhaps jealous Venus has oiled
  Your hair with some opiate drug,
Not choosing her charms should be foiled
  By Lady Elizabeth Mugg.

But ah! why awaken the blaze
  Those bright burning-glasses contain,
Whose lens with concentrated rays
  Proved fatal to old Drury Lane?
'Twas all accidental, they cry –
  Away with the flimsy humbug!
'Twas fired by a flash from the eye
  Of Lady Elizabeth Mugg.

Thy glance can in us raise a flame,
　　Then why should old Drury be free?
Our doom and its doom are the same,
　　Both subject to beauty's decree.
No candles the workmen consumed,
　　When deep in the ruins they dug;
Thy flash still their progress illumed,
　　Sweet Lady Elizabeth Mugg.

Thy face a rich fireplace displays:
　　The mantelpiece marble – thy brows;
Thine eyes are the bright beaming blaze;
　　Thy bib, which no trespass allows,
The fender's tall barrier marks;
　　Thy tippet's the fire-quelling rug,
Which serves to extinguish the sparks
　　Of Lady Elizabeth Mugg.

The Countess a lily appears,
　　Whose tresses the pearl-drops emboss;
The Marchioness blooming in years,
　　A rose-bud enveloped in moss;
But thou art the sweet passion-flower,
　　For who would not slavery hug,
To pass but one exquisite hour
　　In the arms of Elizabeth Mugg?

When at court, or some Dowager's rout,
　　Her diamond aigrette meets our view,
She looks like a glow-worm dressed out,
　　Or tulips bespangled with dew,
Her two lips denied to man's suit
　　Are shared with her favourite Pug;
What lord would not change with the brute,
　　To live with Elizabeth Mugg?

Could the stage be a large vis-à-vis,
    Reserved for the polished and great,
Where each happy lover might see
    The nymph he adores tête-à-tête;
No longer I'd gaze on the ground,
    And load of despondency lug,
For I'd book myself all the year round
    To ride with the sweet Lady Mugg.

Yes, she in herself is a host,
    And if she were here all alone,
Our house might nocturnally boast
    A bumper of fashion and *ton*.
Again should it burst in a blaze,
    In vain would they ply Congreve's plug,
For nought could extinguish the rays
    From the glance of divine Lady Mugg.

O could I as Harlequin frisk,
    And thou be my Columbine fair,
My wand should with one magic whisk
    Transport us to Hanover Square:
St George's should lend us its shrine,
    The parson his shoulders might shrug,
But a licence should force him to join
    My hand in the hand of my Mugg.

Court-plaster the weapons should tip,
    By Cupid shot down from above,
Which, cut into spots for thy lip,
    Should still barb the arrows of love.
The God who from others flies quick,
    With us should be slow as a slug;
As close as a leech he should stick
    To me and Elizabeth Mugg.

For Time would with us, 'stead of sand,
    Put filings of steel in his glass,
To dry up the blots of his hand,
    And spangle life's page as they pass,
Since all flesh is grass ere 'tis hay,
    O may I in clover live snug,
And when old Time mows me away,
    Be stacked with defunct Lady Mugg!

JAMES AND HORACE SMITH

Sally Simpkin's Lament

OR 'JOHN JONES'S KIT-CAT-ASTROPHE'

> He left his body to the sea,
> And made a shark his legatee.
>
> *— Bryan and Perenne.*

'Oh! what is that comes gliding in,
    And quite in middling haste?
It is the picture of my Jones,
    And painted to the waist.

'It is not painted to the life,
    For where's the trowsers blue?
Oh Jones, my dear! – Oh dear! my Jones,
    What is become of you?'

'Oh! Sally dear, it is too true, –
    The half that you remark
Is come to say my other half
    Is bit off by a shark!

'Oh! Sally, sharks do things by halves
    Yet most completely do!
A bite in one place seems enough,
    But I've been bit in two.

'You know I once was all your own,
　　But now a shark must share!
But let that pass – for now to you
　　I'm neither here nor there.

'Alas! death has a strange divorce
　　Effected in the sea.
It has divided me from you,
　　And even me from me.

'Don't fear my ghost will walk o' nights
　　To haunt as people say;
My ghost *can't* walk, for, oh! my legs
　　Are many leagues away!

'Lord! think when I am swimming round,
　　And looking where the boat is,
A shark just snaps away a *half*,
　　Without "a *quarter's* notice"

'One half is here, the other half
　　Is near Columbia placed:
Oh! Sally, I have got the whole
　　Atlantic for my waist.

'But now, adieu – a long adieu!
　　I've solved death's awful riddle.
And would say more, but I am doomed
　　To break off in the middle.'

THOMAS HOOD

A Bad Day by the River

The Overlord of Roaches
   Has made a Royal Rule,
For Roach and Rudd and Loaches
   And fish of pond and pool,
Proclaimed it in the river,
   And nailed it to a tree:
That no fish whatsoever
   Is to be caught by me.

Signed by the King of Roaches
   In this his Royal Stream;
Sealed by the Lord of Loaches;
   Attested by a Bream;
Engrossed by twenty Perches;
   Translated into French;
Read out in all the churches,
   And broadcast by a Tench.

E. V. RIEU

Reflections at Dawn

I wish I owned a Dior dress
   Made to my order out of satin.
I wish I weighed a little less
   And could read Latin,
Had perfect pitch or matching pearls,
   A better head for street directions,
And seven daughters, all with curls
   And fair complexions.
I wish I'd tan instead of burn.
   But most, on all the stars that glisten,
I wish at parties I could learn
   To sit and listen.

I wish I didn't talk so much at parties.
It isn't that I want to hear
My voice assaulting every ear,
Uprising loud and firm and clear
  Above the cocktail clatter.
It's simply, once a doorbell's rung,
(I've been like this since I was young)
Some madness overtakes my tongue
  And I begin to chatter.

Buffet, ball, banquet, quilting bee,
  Wherever conversation's flowing,
Why must I feel it falls on me
  To keep things going?
Though ladies cleverer than I
  Can loll in silence, soft and idle,
Whatever topic gallops by,
  I seize its bridle,
Hold forth on art, dissect the stage,
  Or babble like a kindergart'ner
Of politics till I enrage
  My dinner partner.

I wish I didn't talk so much at parties.
When hotly boil the arguments,
Ah! would I had the common sense
To sit demurely on a fence
  And let who will be vocal,
Instead of plunging in the fray
With my opinions on display
Till all the gentlemen edge away
  To catch an early local.

Oh! there is many a likely boon
  That fate might flip me from her griddle.
I wish that I could sleep till noon
  And play the fiddle,

Or dance a *tour jeté* so light
   It would not shake a single straw down.
But when I ponder how last night
   I laid the law down,
More than to have the Midas touch
   Or critics' praise, however hearty,
I wish I didn't talk so much,
I wish I didn't talk so much,
I wish I didn't talk so much
   When I am at a party.

PHYLLIS McGINLEY

INDEX OF AUTHORS

INDEX OF FIRST LINES

Also published by Penguins:

THE PENGUIN BOOK OF COMIC AND CURIOUS VERSE

YET MORE COMIC AND CURIOUS VERSE

Edited by J. M. Cohen

What the critics have said about the *Comic and Curious* books:

'The widest and most catholic collection that I have met . . . a most diverting and comprehensive anthology' – *Evening News*

'Full of out-of-the-way delights' – *Punch*

'Unusual numbers of good things brought to light' – *The Times Literary Supplement*

'Another pleasantly idiosyncratic blend of the chestnut and the less familiar' – *Observer*

'A splendid book to give those with a bored or too solemn an outlook on poetry' – *Listener*

'Wonderful funny stuff' – *Tribune*

For a complete list of books available please write to Penguin Books whose address can be found on the back of the title page